Freedom From Addiction FAQs

ISBN: 9798678070784

Front cover image by Gerd Altmann from Pixabay.

Back cover image by Arek Socha from Pixabay.

Page design and editing by Vernon Terrell.

Dedication

I dedicate this book to my long-suffering wife, Julia who has loved me unconditionally for the last forty-eight years. You would not be reading this book if it were not for her.

Introduction

In 1990, I was a broken pastor. My church was dying. My church growth plans were spent. My emotions were empty. My mind was confused. My energy was depleted. I was undone. Early in the morning hours on October 6, I was lying on my face in my office crying and praying. I told God that I was giving up on trying to live the Christian life and that I was done with struggling to be a successful pastor. In my utter despair I denounced all my self-effort to try to turn things around in my life and in my church. I told God that I was a blank slate and if He wanted something to take root in me, He would have to be the one to put it there. I was open to anything at that point because what I'd believed and tried certainly had failed me. I asked Him to guide me to the understanding I needed to have.

A few short weeks later, after having received an invitation to attend a conference about grace, I found myself sitting among others in the audience when Mike Quarles stepped up to the podium to speak. Immediately, I was mesmerized by this man. I'd never heard somebody in ministry like him. Mike talked about how he had become addicted to alcohol after graduating from seminary and serving as a pastor. He confessed how it had wrecked his marriage. He spoke honestly about his repeated struggles to be free and the ensuing failures in each attempt.

I remember sitting there in shock that a person in ministry would be so honest, so transparent about such personal things in his life. He talked about how he had rededicated himself to God and promised to do better again and again. He listed many of the treatment programs where he had tried and failed to find the freedom he so desperately wanted.

Then Mike began to show from the Bible the Answer that had set him free. That Answer wasn't grounded in plans, programs and promises but was a Person. The message he shared that day was simultaneously simple and profound.

Something in me woke up that day. Having served as a pastor at that time for seventeen years and having trust Christ as an eight-year-old boy, I was stunned by Mike's simple message of the grace of God expressed in Jesus Christ. It's no exaggeration to say that Mike Quarles was the first person I ever heard teach pure grace. That moment set me on a journey that would transform my own life.
Little did I know at that time that Mike would become, not only a hero, but a good friend. Today it is my pleasure to work with him as he leads the Grace Walk Recovery ministry. Here we are thirty years later and Mike's message is as profound and simple as it was that day I heard him for the first time.
In Freedom From Addiction FAQs, Mike answers the common questions that people have about the message of freedom he teaches. Paradigm shifts don't happen without many "Yes, but . . ." sorts of questions and objections. Mike faces these head on in this book in a way that disarms confusion and resistance to the simple gospel of grace.
   We've all been addicted to something at some time in life. This book is a road-map that will guide the reader to The Way out. Objectors to the message of grace abound but Mike's message isn't on trial. Someone said, "A man with an experience is never at the mercy of a man with an argument." Like another man from long ago, Mike can say, "I once was blind but now I see." It's hard to argue with that kind of experience. His life is the testament to his message. I heartily commend this book to those who search for freedom or know those who do. Read it and share it with the person who comes to your mind because when you know the Truth, the Truth really does set you free.

Steve McVey

Preface

Why Is Addiction So Difficult To Get Free From?

I believe that addiction is the most misunderstood issue that many Christians are facing. I know as I struggled with addiction for eight long nightmarish years after I had graduated from seminary and served in the pastorate. In fact, it was eighteen years after I became a Christian before I found my freedom 32 years ago. During that time, I wanted desperately to be free of my addiction that was destroying everything in my life that was important to me. I struggled with all my might to get free from addiction. I looked for and desperately sought an answer. But with all the many people who tried to sincerely help me I received absolutely no help. I went through a secular treatment center, a Christian treatment center, hundreds of AA meetings and five sponsors, a Christian 12 Step program, Christian counselors and, flew to New Jersey and spent three days with an addictions specialist, secular psychiatrists, psychologists, healing of Memories session, Baptism of Spirit session, casting out of demons session (twice), public confession, group therapy and took the drug Antabuse that if you drink alcohol while on it makes you violently ill. Yes, that happened twice with me. I was disciplined by my church for my drunkenness who sent me to a secular treatment center.

Recently someone called me and wanted an expert on addiction to write an article for an e-magazine he is starting. Well, my wife says I have a D. D., a Doctorate in Drunkenness, so I think I qualify. I have been involved in a recovery ministry of some sort for over 35 years. In fact, I was in a recovery ministry three years before I found my freedom. I struggled with alcoholism for eight long, nightmarish years after graduating from seminary and serving in the pastorate. So, I do know something about how difficult it is to get free from addiction, even for a Christian.

Sometimes I even think it may be harder for a Christian and I will speak to that later on. There is no question that it is a worldwide epidemic. There is no doubt that it is responsible for so much tragedy, trauma, destruction (of families, finances, health, relationships, etc.). The vast majority of people in prison are there because of a drug/alcohol related crime. It seems that most in recovery ministry do not share the answer that we present for addiction. In fact, I know of very few that are based on the answer we present. What is the answer we present? The Answer is that God has provided freedom as Gal. 2:20 clearly lays out for us;

1.   The old person we were has been put to death. Since the person is dead there is nothing that he can do and all they try to do is counter-productive.
2.   It is no longer up to us "as we no longer live as the old self that we were has been crucified with Christ,
3.   Christ lives in us and is our life and we live by faith in the truth that we are dead to sin and freed from it and
4.   The life we now live by faith trusting Christ as our life we live free from addiction.
5.   The finished work of Christ has provided all that we need to live free, victorious lives with peace, joy and fulfillment. There is nothing to do but believe the truth that sets free of who we are in Christ.

Basically, I am saying that God's Answer for addiction has already been provided through the finished work of Christ, i. e. that every born-again believer is dead to sin and freed from it and when we know that we live free from addiction. We are saying that it is all of grace, that God does it all and our only contribution is faith, i.e. to believe the truth of who we are in Christ and that that we are dead to sin and freed from it. Of course, if you go to most recovery ministries they will tell you what you need to do and that it is up to you to do it. That is why so few are finding the freedom that has already been provided for them. I remember that at the Christian Treatment Center I attended the Director told me that "if someone tried to force me to take a drink I should fight it with all my strength even to giving up my life". Well no one has ever tried to force me to take a drink. That really wasn't the problem. In fact, I was all too willing for many years to take not just one drink, but many. I realize he was very sincere in what he was saying, but I believe that mindset and belief is what keeps many people from experiencing the freedom that has already been given to them. When we commit to do what we can to not sin (get drunk, do drugs, have illicit sex, etc.) we are acting in unbelief and saying we don't believe what God says (that we are dead sin and free from it). In other words, we only experience being dead to sin and freed from it and not getting drunk/high by faith. Now the majority of Christians do not struggle with addiction, but as an expert I can tell you that many do. As I said I have been in this type of ministry for 32 years and it keeps me busy. I am convinced that the truth of Gal. 2:20 is what we need to experience peace, freedom and joy, but it really does seem that most do not have a clear understanding of it. I certainly did not even though I was a seminary graduate, pastor and considered myself a biblical student (not a scholar). It wasn't until 1988 after I had been struggling for eight years that I heard Bill Gillham teach on Romans 6 that I understood grace and that I was dead to sin, freed from it and who I was in Christ. That knowledge freed me from my addiction. However, it seems that most Christians, not knowing these truths get along okay and are not brought to the point I was where death was an enviable prospect and I was totally convinced that there was absolutely nothing I could do to get free of the addiction. Now I run into a lot of people like this because of my ministry. But I would have to say that it doesn't seem that most Christians get to that point. Looking back, I can honestly say that I consider myself very fortunate to have been there. I would not be experiencing the peace, freedom and joy I am if I hadn't got to that point. What was the point that I had reached? The Apostle Paul describes it We do not want you to be uninformed, brothers, about the hardships we suffered in the province of Asia. We were under great pressure, far beyond our ability to endure, so that we despaired even of life. Indeed, in our hearts we felt the sentence of death. But this happened that we might not rely on ourselves but on God, who raises the dead. (2 Cor. 1:8, 9). Would you agree that is the point where God can get our attention? However, most Christians do everything they can not to get to that point. Neil Anderson has said that the day of his brokenness was the best day of his life. I agree completely as that is the day both Neil and myself found our freedom (not to mention the ministry I have had for the last 32 years and that Neil has had for over 50 years. Neil Anderson was the founder of Freedom in Christ Ministries and it is responsible for many thousands finding their freedom in Christ. I was privileged to work with Neil in that ministry for twelve years and co-authored four books with him on freedom from addiction.

Lately I have been thinking that for anyone who is struggling with an addiction to get free must get to that point of coming to the end of self and his resources. But that is to just come to the place where you are forced to turn to God and find His Answer for addiction. The actual experiential deliverance comes when we know and believe the truth of Gal. 2:20. I am convinced that we must know

1) the old person we were is dead and gone and can do nothing.
2) It is not up to us to do anything because Christ lives in us and is living our life.
3) We can now live by faith in the truth (fact) that we are dead to sin and freed from it (addiction).
4) As we live by faith trusting Christ as our life we live free from addiction in peace, freedom and joy.
5) There is absolutely nothing to do as the old self is dead

and gone and Christ is our life.

My point in all of this is that it would appear that most Christians do not seem to understand the reality of Gal. 2:20 and it doesn't appear to have that much of an adverse effect on them. Oh, they go through all the trials, troubles and trauma that life brings to all of us, but not the devastation and desolation that alcohol/drug/sex addiction and other addictions brings to people like me. My conclusion is that the only hope for people like me (and possibly you or a loved one or friend) is to really understand and know that Christ in us is the hope of glory, that Christ is our life and the life we are living we live by faith of the Son of God who loved us and gave Himself for us. Does this mean that we are second class Christians doomed to struggle and grovel along in this life? No, on the contrary I thank God and praise Him for my half a century of struggling and the misery, despair and devastation I suffered (I was 51 when I got free). Why? Because for the last 32 years I have experienced true and lasting freedom in Christ from addiction. Oh, I have had my ups and downs and I am not the perfect husband and Christian as my wife can give testimony. But I have been free from addiction for 32 years. it has been my great privilege and blessing to be in ministry and point people to the Son who when He sets you free you are free indeed (John 8:36). I believe it is not just receiving Him and I received Christ 50 years ago. But it is knowing what you get and who you are and what has happened. And for 18 years I just understood that my sins were forgiven and I had eternal life, was going to heaven and Jesus was my Lord and Savior. Now that's pretty good but I was taught and understood that it was up to me to do what I needed to do to get Jesus to bless me, free me, help me, provide for me, protect me, heal me, be with me, etc. etc.

I really had no concept that He was my life and was living it and all the stumbling, fumbling, faltering, and failing was part of His living His life in me to show me who He was in me and who I was in Him and what I had in Him. It took eight years of living in a nightmare of addiction that I couldn't wake up from to get a glimpse of Christ in me, the hope of glory. And that glimpse was enough to free me from my addiction. That was 32 years ago and I am still learning, receiving, and letting Christ live His life in me. It is not a life lived on a bed of roses, but with all the thorns intact as I like you live in a body that is falling apart and in a fallen world in which Satan is the ruler. The trials, troubles and trauma continue. But so, what? We have it all. We have the ALL IN ALL in us. I have Christ in me. I have everything. I am invincible. I am bulletproof. No, it sure doesn't feel like it, but it is still true.

When I started this there was a point I wanted to make and I'm not sure if I did. The point is that people like me who have and/or struggling with an alcohol/drug and/or sex addiction or any other addictive behavior are not going to find freedom until they know Christ as life (not just Lord and Savior). There is a monumental difference between knowing Him as a Savior (out there) who saves us and a Lord we submit to (separate from us) and knowing that He is my very life and He is living my life. WOW! SELAH (Pause and think about that). Whoa! How can it be? Only by a miracle and only by grace and that miracle has taken place in you and me. Will you believe it? Will you receive it? The 100+ questions that follow are actual questions that were asked of me. Most of them were in emails, some personal, some on the phone and quite a few of them were in the webinars that we conduct and at the end open it up for a Q & A.

I have been asked a lot of questions about freedom from addiction that God has provided. I have responded to them and answered them. There is a worldwide epidemic and no one seems to have an answer. But God has provided an answer. Christians have a lot of questions such as "How do I make this true in my life?", "What about AA and the 12 Steps?", "What do you mean that the Church has bought a lie about addiction?" In this book is a list of questions where you will find the answers. The secular has no clue as to what the problem or the answer for addiction is. That is not to say that the secular hasn't given it their best shot and their most informed and educated guess. But the world doesn't have access to the true answer. That is only available to those who have a personal relationship with the God of the universe through His Son, the Redeemer, the Lord Jesus Christ. But by and large the church doesn't seem to have grasped the answer either. I struggled with alcoholism and didn't find an answer until after I had been a Christian for eighteen years. I sought long, hard and very diligently, but no one pointed me to the "the truth that sets free". I finally found my freedom from alcoholism 32 years ago after living through a nightmare of hell for eight years as I listened to a message on a tape on Romans 6. I had been told countless things to do and tried them all to no avail. But that day as I heard the truth that I was dead to sin and freed from it (Rom. 6:6, 7) I was freed from my addiction and have been for the last 32 years. What did I do?!? **ABSOLUTELY NOTHING!** As a matter of fact, I had a hangover and was driving in a car and couldn't do anything. I simply believed the truth of Gal. 2:20, *I have been crucified with Christ and I no longer live, but Christ lives in me. The life I live in the body, I live by faith in the Son of God, who loved me and gave himself for me.*

FAQs

#	Question	Page
1	This is a query from a friend of mine who is an exchanged life counselor who asked me what I thought about a secular authority's take on addiction.	1
2	How did it (your freedom) happen for you?	2
3	But haven't you grown and matured in your freedom over the years?	3
4	What do you mean that the church doesn't know what the problem and answer for addiction is?	3
5	Why do you say that most pastors and counselors don't understand what the answer for addiction is?	5
6	Don't you think AA, 12-Step programs, secular treatment, and Christian treatment can help in the process to get free?	6
7	If we are really free, shouldn't we be able to drink alcohol in moderation?	7
8	What about AA?	7
9	What is the church (the evangelical community) missing?	9
10	I have been diagnosed as bipolar. Does that mean I have to live with it the rest of my life?	11
11	What do you mean when you say we must come to brokenness before we can believe the truth that sets free?	12
12	Do you think the problem with Christians struggling with an addictive behavior is that they are not born again?	13
13	How do you explain the fact that Brennan Manning the famous Catholic priest, and noted author never got totally free of his addiction to alcoholism and died from complications of it?	13
14	When listening to the webinars, my wife and I heard people ask this same type of questions time and again. Perhaps it's because people struggle with the concept of grace by faith. Perhaps you can begin to share what people can do to build their faith so they can better understand how much God loves them. And I'm not talking about works. I'm talking about the bi-product of faith practiced anytime you are interested in building a relationship. In other words, not all doing/living is "works."	15
15	I am currently in recovery for an addiction and it really bothers me to hear the leader of an on-line ministry that I'm a part of continue to refer to herself and others, years after recovery, still	

as addicts, and also subscribes to the idea of "once an addict always an addict". I find it self-defeating and discouraging to hear the gospel and Christ's work on the cross negated in this way, as though what Christ did isn't enough. I'd like to hear your thoughts on this. 16

16   What part does the demonic play in addiction? 17

17   What about casting out demons through a power encounter? 19

18   Isn't it a sin to drink wine (or have a beer or two)?.....................20

19   Do we have an evil heart or a good heart after we receive Christ?...20

20   Is this sin ("using" on a daily basis) what's keeping me from drawing close to Jesus? Do I need to obey his commandments more so to feel his presence?...22

21   How do I appropriate Christ as life that I know and believe I have? 23

22   How can I figure out how to be free?...25

23   In your Overcomer's Covenant in Christ #1 of the Covenant you say that "such programs and groups can be very caring, and may result in abstinence from alcohol and drugs, but ultimately salvation and freedom can only come in Christ." My question is, what is the ultimate difference between abstinence vs freedom in Christ or the freedom that Jesus gives? For a food addict does that mean that person can eat a doughnut and not worry about it causing this person to binge on other foods for example? Or an alcoholic who is free by Jesus Christ, can they have one glass of beer or wine and not go off and get drunk? 26

24   What about Celebrate Recovery? 27

25   What can I do to get free and live the victorious Christian life?....28

26   What keeps us from living the abundant, victorious life that is ours in Christ? Satan? Well, yes, but how does he do it? What is his weapon that is so powerful? Of course it is the lie, but how many of us realize that and do anything about it as we falter, fumble and fail in life as I've spent too much of my life doing. Why is the lie so effective?..30

27   How Can I Believe the Truth that sets free? 33

28   Hyper-Grace!?!?...37

29   If a person is an alcoholic, then he must not be a Christian. Is that not so? 41

30   I have never gotten to the point where I feel that Christ is my life

and I am living it. I have been so strong at times and so weak at others. I just don't get it?...45

31   What if a person is a lesbian? Homosexual? 46

32   Why do you say that Gal. 2:20 is the key and when people understand and believe it is when they get free?.........................47

33   I have already watched the Fireproof Movie twice since it arrived. What stands out to me is selfishness! I have been SO selfish with my wife, especially in the area of EXPECTING her to gratify me physically. Then as I was going back to the Love Dare devotional, I realized that on the first 2 attempts, a few years ago, I was just faking it. My heart was not ALL IN. I was just going thru' it getting my checks in the boxes and not giving God and His Spirit the chance to transform me. It seemed like I needed to "camp out" a whole week on the first 2 days of Patience and Kindness. Then as I was talking to my wife last night, she told me straight out that what she was looking for in a loving husband was: Patience and Kindness. A lot of times this prideful idiot (me) needs to be hit over the head with a baseball bat to get it. And this was the Holy Spirit's gentle "baseball bat", confirming thru' my wife's direct words to focus on Patience & Kindness to develop my character.48

34   Do you not believe that drinking alcohol is a sin? Many teach that it is?...53

35   How can we be filled with the Spirit and not get drunk? 54

36   It has been awhile since I reached out to you about my marriage and our separation. It appears my husband sees no future for us except "hopelessness". A friend of mine asked me to research "narcissism" and WOW... most of the characteristics are classic. Have you dealt with this and is it likely he can or will change? I realize that is a blanket question and probably a bit unfair, but have you had any dealings with this? 55

37   What does it mean to "believe"?..56

38   Up to this point, not one of the few people to whom I have proclaimed this truth has been set free. I am feeling that this truth must be revealed to each individual by the Holy Spirit. We have prayed and proclaimed, but is it not true this requires the individual to cast themselves upon Christ in such a manner that they are desperately dependent on His working and solely trusting that He alone can deliver them??? 57

39   I've struggled with an addiction for a looooonnnnng time and while I have had days of freedom, I have never had a consistent total victory. I have tried everything and even did your on-line

webinar, but still...no joy. Joseph Prince, in his book "The Power of Right Believing", basically teaches that "we are the righteousness of God in Christ Jesus" and that if we keep confessing that we will eventually get freedom. I have run out of options and every time I hear something "new" that I haven't tried I think to myself that this is it, I will finally get free, only to be disappointed. Is there still any hope for me? 59

40   What about the physical aspect of addiction? I believe that my smoking is an addiction. Doesn't the physical aspect of addiction have to be addressed? 60

41   What about casting out a demon? Don't you believe that the demonic is involved in addiction and that a "power encounter" is needed?...61

42   What about prescription meds? I am on antidepressants and thinking about getting off them by going cold turkey. What would be your advice on this?...62

43   I am addicted to pain medication (Oxycontin). These are prescribed and without them I am in severe pain. But here is my dilemma, I do not know if the Lord wants me to give these pain meds up or not? The obvious answer is: "Ask God." But, I have and I am just not sure I am hearing from Him or not. Since asking Him, I have been reading a lot about 'idols' and also repentance. Then I try to go off them and the excruciating pain sets in and I return to taking them and at the same time, as a result of my long term illness, my life has fallen apart. I have other health issues that are so debilitating that without pain meds I would be bedridden. But I keep on having to up my dose or they don't work. Seems like they are a horrible lie from Satan. I have been like this for five years and most of my relationships have not survived and my home is under threat of the bank. 63

44   You quote John 8:32 a lot "Then you will know the truth, and the truth will set you free." But what about John 8:31 that says if you continue in the word then you will know the truth. Don't those two verses go together?..65

45   It seems to me that the reason for people struggling with addictive behavior is that they have not grown and matured in the Christian life and do not understand and know what will bring joy in their life. 66

46   It seems you don't recognize the demonic factor in addiction and downplay spiritual warfare. Don't you think the demonic should be addressed? 67

47   I have read in a devotional by a famous author to pray, read the

bible, memorize scripture, go to church, and resist temptation and I will eventually get free from my addiction. Are you saying that this will not help?..68

48 What are the four strongholds of addiction and where do you find that in scripture?..70

49 I believe my husband is an alcoholic. He doesn't drink every day but is a binge drinker. When he is not drinking everything is OK and we get along well. What would you recommend that I do?..74

50 Does the church have an answer for addiction?............................75

51 Do you think I'm wrong in saying that a person struggling with an addiction is not born again and a believer in Christ?..................76

52 What about going to a treatment center??...................................77

53 You really emphasize grace to the extent that there is nothing for us to do, but believe that God has done it all. Surely there is something we need to be doing such as prayer, bible study and reading, etc. to get our freedom and maintain it, isn't it?............78

54 You asked at the webinar if I had ever been tempted to go back to my addiction and I said no. That is true, but I believe I need to clarify that. 80

55 I have developed my own plan of intensive study, diet, exercise, vitamins, journaling and talking and listening to the Lord over the next three months as if I were in a treatment center. What do you think? 82

56 How can I know the will of God? If I can figure it out, then I believe it would enable me to live in freedom and victory. 84

57 Christianity Today has reported that virtually all Christian recovery ministries are based on the 12 Steps. Why is this?.....................84

58 I went through your webinars several times. It's been about a year and a half, and it's truly amazing that I'm free. What chaps me the most though is I've been free for 30 years and just didn't know it. One thing I found was that after I received the revelation that I died and that I no longer live but Christ is my life, I would try to live in the sensation of that revelation. This feeling would slowly pass and I found myself doubting who I really was in Christ. It took some time, but I don't need to feel free. I am free. That was the turning point. You will know the truth and the truth will set you free. It's that word "know" that was key for me. Thank you, Mike. 86

59 You talk often about Romans 6:14, "we are not under law, but under grace". I totally agree. What do you do then with all the

commands Paul gives in that same book (especially chapters 12-15) and at the end of most of his epistles? Do you see a difference between these commands and law? 87

60 On your last email, you said nothing to do to maintain? Apparently, I believed on March 31 and experienced my freedom. As I have said before I have experienced my freedom many times, but it does not last. How did your freedom last and mine always wither away? Why am I struggling to BELIEVE again? What happened to the believing faith I exercised on March 31? Did I stop believing? If so, how do I start back believing? Why am I only experiencing the same old, same old life as usual? What happened to the victory, the peace, the joy? I have been listening again and again to the webinars and you and Vernon keep saying only believe. How do I keep on believing? What is pulling me off the believing? When you found your freedom, did you ever lose it, regain it, lose it again?   If not, what's wrong with my believing?.88

61 Do you ever experience fear, anxiety, worry, stress? If so, what do you do when it comes to you?..90

62 A gracious thank you for the 3 disk CD Freedom From Addictive Behaviors. You have even personally replied to my emails. I can't even tell you how much that has impacted me. I'm still smoking heroin but I think I'm afraid because after I go to a medical detox for 5 or 7 days I'm great and the withdrawals are gone. Hard part done. But what if my wanting to use again is greater than my wanting to be free? Or sober, in other words. I'm telling you it's gonna take a miracle for MY mind to NOT want to smoke heroin..91

63 Why do addicts lie and manipulate others?...................................93

64 My husband is an unbeliever and has absolutely no interest in God. He is also an alcoholic and has zero interest in quitting. Is it possible to live in love with an unbeliever? 94

65 Do you think there is any value in going to school to be Christian counselor or a pastor or a Christian family therapist? If identity is key...what about finding financial provision and a job you like? Is that part of freedom in Christ? 96

66 How would you get involved in professional ministry? Or just avoid that all together? 97

67 You have shared that your ministry has not been well received and that many do not respond to it. How do you feel about that?.....98

68 I have watched all your webinars and read your material. I agree with everything you teach. Unfortunately, I am still bound in

overeating. I'm not sure why I am not finding freedom. Do you have any testimonies of people being freed from an addiction to overeating?...99

69   Thank you so very much for your testimony and hard work in putting these webinars together. You guys do a wonderful job. Unfortunately, I still have the chains of alcohol pulling me down in a deep dark pit. I have no self-control in this area. Over 10 years of continuous up and down, start and stop. I have a job and family and manage to survive but am sick of this lifestyle. My wife has no idea about this ongoing struggle. She helped me through this a few years ago, but I started drinking again and now it seems to be my best friend/worse enemy. "As a dog returns to his vomit...". Thank you for letting me share this with you. In fact, you are the only one I have shared this with in many years.?.......................100

70   I have been thinking about your request to hear from people set free from overeating and trying to decide whether or not to respond. I would love to talk with you about it. My hesitation is that even after 20-plus years of involvement and teaching about freedom in Christ and experiencing significant freedom in other areas of my life, this one continued to plague me. 15 years ago I found freedom from this bondage for a year and a half. I even called and talked with you about it at that time because I had questions. But then I lost it. I have very recently been experiencing significant freedom again from overeating, but because of past experience have not shared about it. I know this freedom is available long term and hope to share more about the victory. Both times it has been a new understanding and BELIEF IN particular verses from Romans 6 that impacted me. I know that's no surprise. This time 6:11 "...consider yourselves..."! I guess I didn't quite believe ..."I can! ...because...". 102

71   My youngest son is finishing up a year program at Teen Challenge. Our middle son went through a similar struggle six or seven years ago. The ripple effect of all of this is that I still struggle not to enable him (not financially, not with school, but in other ways) - because I want him to be better. And I do feel responsible for much of his problems with addiction for a number of reasons. My husband can attest that I didn't want him to struggle in school, so I took on his issues all the time. I was pretty much a helicopter parent who wanted to fix every problem, make things better, and make up for the time spent away from him at work, with his brothers - etc. And my biggest fear that I am still hanging on to is - what if he relapses and leaves and we never see him again. I know it sounds crazy to be afraid of what hasn't happened. So, the thing is - other people notice this (especially his older brother)

- who told me yesterday that he doesn't even like talking to me about his brother because it feels like my whole life is centered around what he does and doesn't do. And my husband agreed I struggle with this. He said - "the things you do, you listen to their sermons, you listen to their music - just to feel like you are a part of what he is doing." So, I guess I need to re-read your book, because even though it is my son with the "addiction problem" that you can see, I have had and have a different problem. I am addicted to being the "fixer mom". Only - when I do this, I am not seeing that the result is pushing people I love further and further away. And the person I am trying to "fix" also is uncomfortable by it all. The thoughts of "see it's your fault he has these problems" --- continue to attack my thinking - even though I know the truth of the Gospel. And shame and blame are never a helpful, productive thing. The "what ifs" are so frustrating to deal with. So, before I can be a good helper to anyone overcoming addiction, my prayer is that the Lord shows me my real problem. That He works in the garden of my heart and uproots those things I have been struggling with and hanging onto. Things that keep me from fully living in the free abundant life that is mine daily in Jesus Christ. I do not want to be that enabler mom any longer. I want to rest in grace, truth and peace. 103

72   I was looking up a quote from last week's webinar from Martin Luther. Do you gather that this gent has "rewritten" Luther's Galatians introduction in an accurate manner? 106

73   Obviously, clinical addictions to drugs, porn, alcohol, etc., are powerful deterrents to the abundant life Jesus promised. It's just that when those addictions are the focus, it plays into the con that all the other people who aren't terrorized by those addictions are somehow free. Satan has duped the whole world and almost 100% of so-called Christians that they are all addicted (bound) to their flesh. I wish you guys would broaden your focus and help break this con that is being perpetrated on all men. 107

74   This is rather a long question, but it gets right to the heart of the matter considering the problem and the answer for addiction. Mike, we have seen a number of men and women freed from addiction to drugs, porn, and alcohol here. We make sure that they know who they are in Christ and that they are no longer self-identified as addicts. Something came up the other evening in a meeting. One of the people there said that a person who has come to Christ and knows the truth of who they are in Christ is no longer an addict. That addiction ceases. I tended to disagree in part. I was reading yours and Steve McVey's book "Helping Others Overcome Addictions" and I came across a quote from a

lady who said this: "I was set free by understanding who I am in Christ....I told (my group) 'I am not an alcoholic by nature! I am a righteous child of God who has a physical and psychological vulnerability toward alcohol abuse, but that isn't what defines me.....'" (p. 133). My take on what she says and my understanding of what it means to be "in Christ" is that the person who is an abuser of drugs, alcohol, porn, etc. has little ability to refrain from that abusive addiction before accepting Christ; however, after coming to Jesus, the Holy Spirit works in them so that they do have the ability to refrain, but that they must "die daily" to any desire. The Holy Spirit empowers them to do so. My disagreement is that for some, perhaps many, going back to the source of the abuse (drugs, alcohol, etc.) may send them on a spiral back toward their own self-abuse from whence they came. In other words, because of that "physical and psychological vulnerability" their addiction can return. Therefore, a person, for example, who had an addiction to alcohol but has gained legitimate freedom in Christ cannot go into a bar with friends and have a couple of drinks without the strong possibility that he or she may return to the same behavior as experienced before coming to freedom. So would it be fair to say that someone had freedom from addiction, but because of being physically and psychologically vulnerable, they may be always subject to addiction if they return to the

source? 108

75   I wrote to you a couple of days ago, but I think I had a breakthrough yesterday where I am beginning to understand what you're saying about the old self being crucified with Christ. As I mentioned before, I have wrestled with depression and despair for many years, and I currently wake up during the night each night and a bolt of anxiety instantly surges through me. But last night I just kept saying, "That's not who I am. That old self that worries and fears and panics has been crucified with Christ. It is dead and powerless. I have been crucified with Christ, and it is no longer I who live, but Christ who lives in me." I said that over and over, and I had peace amidst the storm and went back to sleep faster than usual. I realized that I have spent a lot of time and energy trying to fix, control, or numb my sinful flesh, in an effort to get rid of sinful thoughts altogether. But I can't do that. Nothing works. I just have to accept that my sinful flesh exists on this earth and it will try hard to annoy and harass me, but my comfort and peace is in knowing, really knowing that it has been crucified and buried, and it is powerless. When I have irrational anxious thoughts or powerful feelings of sadness, those are from the part of me that has died and I can dismiss them as such. I have tried over and

over to discipline myself to think positive thoughts, to be thankful, to ask for forgiveness, but nothing has seemed to work and I have plunged deeper and deeper into despair. I have tried various medications to try to numb myself or think more positively, but that either doesn't work or I just feel numb altogether. I think that is what you mean by trying to fix the sinful flesh. It can't be done. It is only when I accept the truth that I can't fix myself and that my sinful self has already died, that I can have peace through what Christ has done for me. I can't stop sinful thoughts from entering my brain or impulses from surging through my body, but I don't have to try to fix or eliminate them--that just makes things worse. Just believe the truth that they are not me; I am a new creation. I think this is applying the truths that you've taught, and I will continue thinking about them. Thank you for taking the time to explain the gospel and what it means for us. This is a new understanding for me. 111

76 I'm still teaching the "Helping Others" course. Can you please clarify the statement on the last slide of part 5 that says anything is permissible? I understand that nothing we do can separate us from Christ, but how do I explain and clarify this particular statement better? 113

77 I have had anxiety/depression/OCD for at least 25 years. My childhood involved emotional/sexual/mental abuse and a lot of neglect. Both parents expected perfection (and punished when I wasn't) and my mom often said, "what is wrong with you" and "you should be ashamed of yourself". I do not consciously blame them because I know they did the best they could. I've been to many counselors, prayer sessions, inner healings, etc, etc. and been a believer since I was 5 or 6 years old. I struggle with feeling guilty most of the time and have crazy high expectations of myself. I feel a lot of shame and, of course, think I should have all this together by now and be much closer to perfection than I am at this point. I am on medication now that prevents the dangerously high anxiety and dangerously low depression as I was very ready to end it all early this fall because I saw no hope of ever getting to the other side of this and/or ever really knowing the love of God. I have prayed at least a thousand times to know His love and feel like a child of His. I know ours is not supposed to be an experiential religion all the time, but I KNOW I am supposed to feel SOMETHING and certainly not feel like a guilty slave. Oh, I feel very often that I have to do this or that in order for God to help me be healed. Read this book, listen to this course, pray this prayer, be obedient in this, etc., etc. 115

78 I have been a Christian for nearly a decade and am battling some

addictive problems. I have done everything I know to get free and am not sure how to. I have talked with some Christian leaders and they either have just given me pet answers and sent me on my way, or didn't seem to know what to do. I have been trying to resist not giving up, because I am afraid that if I reach out more, then I will just keep running into the same walls. I am starting to get desperate, because I truly love God and want to serve Him and pursue holiness, but I am really battle weary. Please feel free to contact me on my phone, or by email when you have some free time. Thank you. 117

79   What About the 12 Steps? What's not covered in the 12 steps that is essential to freedom? What's Wrong with The 12 Steps? 118

80   Ok, I will ask my team about the devotional. We all have the Helping Others Overcome Addiction Book. And most of us have read it. What resources do you recommend to conduct the recovery class? 119

81   I had emailed you a couple of months ago about starting a recovery ministry in our church. You recommended that we do the Freedom from Addictive Behaviors Conference DVD's. We have one more session to do. What do you recommend we do next? Are we ready to start a class? If so, what resources would you recommend we use? 120

82   I am so confused. I am stuck in addiction to prescription drugs and bingeing. I have tried to live out who I am in Christ, but I can't help feeling that a group of believers with me is needed for support. Am I to be a Lone Ranger? I have struggled most of my life. How do I get myself to believe, especially when I have such a bad track record? I'm not sure I understand how I stop myself when I go to reach for more pills. Please help me understand. I have tried everything-Neil Anderson's book, deliverance ministry, Bible studies, 12-step meetings, hospitalization. I feel hopeless. 120

83   I know you mean well by what you are teaching, but I am clean and sober 45 years, and from that day have dedicated my life to helping others do it also. I have done a lot of street ministry working with the mentally ill, the addicts and the down and outers. I had a Christian Men's home for many years. I have never tried to make money doing it. That was a promise I made to God before I even knew if he was really there. It was A.A. that saved my life, and it was through them where I started understanding there is a higher power. It took my 23 more years before I gave my life to Christ and knew for sure there was a God. Your method of teaching may work for some. However, we do not all get the

great awakening at once. For many of us it takes time. I have spent many hours detoxing guys in motel rooms. I would never, ever try drinking again. I do not believe in testing God. When I made a statement on your webinar, you blew off my opinion as if I knew nothing. We are all different people with different ways of seeing things, and different needs. You stated that you have a beer at times. Maybe you were not really an alcoholic. I was a fetal alcohol baby. My dad gave me a sip of beer when I was very young, and I remember the anger I had when he took it away. Dad died when I was 15. I drank daily from the age of 15 to 23, searching for the ultimate high, but always passed out before I got there. I understand now the ultimate high to me was death. I had 2 suicide attempts in my last year of drinking. Finally, I had to make the decision do I live or die. My detox was one of the worst experiences in my life. I have since had 22 heart surgeries/ procedures over the last 32 years. I have always found that I have to try to understand each individual who wants help, before God can use me to help that person. There is no one way that will help everyone. Thank you for listening. 122

84 Thanks for sharing your story. I had 30 years of drinking, the last 10 years as a daily drinker. I have been in AA, keeping sober, growing spiritually, reasonably happy and useful for nearly 9 years. I discovered FICM and your website recently through a Christian friend and accountability partner. You are no doubt aware that AA's position in regards to people who have genuinely been addicted to alcohol is "once an alcoholic, always an alcoholic" and that absolute abstinence is the only answer. My question after reading your site and the FICM pages: is the AA position correct, or is a "cure" through Christ and following your steps actually possible. Thanks in advance for your answer. 125

85 Blessings and praise God for your ministry. I am a Christian but also a functioning alcoholic. It has ruined most of my life—I'm now 51 and just about rock bottom. Any attempt I have made to follow your truthful and biblical advice is usually swept away by a tidal wave of remorse and regret at what I have lost and never really had. I wonder if you have any advice for dealing with this overwhelming burden of sadness and hopelessness and regret over my past actions. The cares of each day just sweep me under and I cannot see Christ. 128

86 I am writing for your counsel, please. I am a licensed social worker who practices biblical counseling, and I use Neil Anderson's "Steps to Freedom" in my practice. I am presently working with a 49-year-old man who has been addicted to cocaine since the age of 13. He has 4 children and has been separated often from

his wife in the last 20 years that they have been married (he is the one who leaves). He was raped by a man shortly before he started using and blames this event for his addiction. The Lord supernaturally delivered him from cocaine in the month of May of this year, which is when I began to work with the family (through the school system because of the impact the marital conflict was having on the children). It soon became apparent that he was dealing with many issues that presented as rage and anxiety. He has difficulty understanding the need for accountability and discipleship and did not follow through on the tasks he agreed to work on in the course of our sessions together (individual, couple and family meetings). He believes he is born again. He had a relapse 3 weeks ago and has avoided meeting with me since then. His wife is at her wit's end and is ready to divorce him but is waiting on God for supernatural intervention because she does not want to give up on him or their marriage. I have followed your webinar and I remember how you highlighted the importance of consequences, which your wife upheld, that helped you make a decision for freedom. This is not how he and his wife have functioned in the past. He came and went as he pleased without consequences. His pastor is of the opinion that he needs deliverance and that his will is overtaken by demonic forces which makes it impossible for him to choose freedom and has asked his wife to pray and fast for him. I am of the opinion that he can even in his relapsed state choose to submit to God and seek accountability. Please advise. 130

87 I'm frustrated and am feeling the negative effects of the smoking. My thought is to throw the cigs away (have done sooo may times) and trust God...although I go and buy a pack again. I do have Chantrex, patches, and gum. I feel like I'm in rebellion. Just wanted to share. I'll continue to re-listen to the videos. 132

88 My problem now is I don't see old self crucified. Why? I experienced this crucifixion with Christ about 25 years ago. Don't know what happened to it or how to get it to operate again in my life? What is wrong? 133

89 How can I experience my freedom and not experience Christ as my life? I want to be free indeed, the whole thing, all of it. 134

90 I know for sure I'm going to have to set boundaries when I get out (of prison). I have a great family, a very big family, and they all live close by and have get-togethers all the time where there is drinking; nothing that's out of control, but I just know that just as I've had to set boundaries in here, I will have to do the same out there walking very wisely day by day! 135

91 Just discovered your website; seems like a great ministry. I was in bondage/addiction for many, many years (freedom only through Christ's unconditional grace, love, forgiveness, and mercy). With 60 years of wrong thinking and believing, it is a continual reprogramming process through Christ. 136

92 I'm loving the content. I just stumbled upon this somehow through Facebook. I have been reading through some of your archives and some stuff is really resonating with me. Awesome stuff. The truth has been the only thing that has freed me from addiction. Learning who I am in Christ has definitely impacted my life. Thanks for the confirmation that I was not crazy. LOL. I have opposed some drug counselors last year through a post and was basically shunned because I believe that addiction is basically a symptom of a much bigger problem like you mentioned in one of your blogs. They didn't like that idea at all. These are counselors that are putting people's lives in their hands. They sweep the statistics under the rug and deny the recidivism rates to keep their positions. I was an addict ever since I was eight years old and I'm 47 now, I've been through every program known to man and the only thing that actually freed me was learning who I am in Christ, and even still then I sometimes went back to that addiction in my immaturity. But no secular counseling or rehabilitation center worked ever on me. In fact, when my parents insurance ran out they early graduated me. Go figure. 136

93 You have said that you have a list of over 100 Christians treatment centers? Don't you recommend that Christians should go to one? 138

94 How can you say the Christian treatment you attended and others as well were Christ-centered, but you would not necessarily recommend it? 138

95 Since I talked with you things have gotten worse. She's now in the hospital on a mental health hold. I don't know if they'll release her to treatment or just release her. It's such a helpless feeling. I am reading the "Helping Others Overcome Addictions" and I believe it. I just don't know if she is ready to accept her identity in Christ yet. You went to treatment a couple of times. Do you think you could have accepted your identity and the finished work on the cross earlier had you known? Or was the process you went through necessary and then also the revelation of the truth by the Holy Spirit. 139

96 Hi Mike....., I have spoken with you before. Your testimony resonates with me because they are so similar. I was in the insurance business for a number of years before going to seminary

to get a degree in pastoral counseling. When I got my degree, I began a ministry in counseling that God really honored and I was asked to speak at many churches in our area. That continued for a number of years until I started having trouble sleeping. My doctor at the time prescribed a very high dose of Xanax, which worked wonders, but eventually made me very depressed. After tying 21 different antidepressant medications, I just decided to go back to my college years and use alcohol to help me. And it did! A very good job. But like you, it has caused me a whole host of problems with family, church, and ministry. Like you, I have tried treatment, counseling, prayer, fasting, etc., etc, etc! But here is my problem. I've read all the material you have sent me and I have read all of Neil's books, even led others through the steps to freedom with success, but I have not found that freedom!!!! It's not like I don't understand the process and believe that it is true; for some reason, it doesn't work for me!! I would like to talk to you again, if possible. 140

97 I have heard you say that God uses everything in our life for good, even all our sins, failures, mistakes, suffering, literally EVERYTHING. Do you really believe that and can you give me a good example of that? 141

98 I'm struggling a bit. My daughter came out of detox yesterday and she didn't go to residential housing. She is living at my house. I feel I've done everything wrong so far. I have an extra car that she can drive to meetings. She has to go 5 days a week from 9 to 3. She is supposed to go to 5 AA or Celebrate Recovery meetings a week. I thought I would only let her have the car for those commitments but I ended up letting her take it to Verizon to get a replacement phone for the one she 'lost'. She doesn't have access to her money, so I paid her initial payment of $170. Now I'm regretting that. She had insurance on the old phone so it didn't have to be a total new purchase of a phone. I didn't think about the fact that she won't have money to pay the next payment without me. Now my struggle is this. Should I say she can't have the car and take her to the classes myself that she has to attend during the day and meetings at night or just let her drive my extra car? If she was using alcohol now and not in treatment, I would know that she couldn't have that freedom. But, since she is in treatment, should I help her in these ways? So, I guess I don't know if Chapter 8 in "Helping Others Overcome Addictions" on what not to do only applies when the person is refusing treatment. 142

99 What do you mean by "the truth that sets free"? 143

100 Why is it so important for addicts/alcoholics to be completely honest about their situation? 144

101 How do we learn "how" to get free? 145

102 With addiction pandemic in the world and getting worse every day "are we missing something"? 145

103 What if someone is really motivated but needs some help in appropriating their freedom, would you recommend working through "The Freedom from Addiction Workbook"? 147

104 Do you recommend "interventions" and if so, could you give me a few guidelines? 148

105 What about repentance? Isn't that essential to finding freedom? 153

106 Is there a "key" to being free and living in victory? Could you give me a list of all the verses you use about freedom? 154

107 You have quoted Madame Guyon who said, "Everything is Jesus. Everything else is a lie." What does that mean? 157

108 Appendix: The Strange Odyssey of a Legalistic Preacher Who Became a Drunk, Discovered Grace and Was Set Free. Mike Quarles' Testimony of Freedom from Addiction 161

"I know now, Lord, why you utter no answer. You are yourself the answer. Before your face questions die away. What other answer would suffice?"
—C.S. Lewis

This is a query from a friend of mine who is an exchanged life counselor who asked me what I thought about a secular authority's take on addiction.

I've been wondering why you found it terribly interesting. I certainly didn't. But maybe it is because I've read so much along that line in years past. I've read books on the history of AA and the 12 Steps, a biography on Bill Wilson (co-founder of AA), who became heavily involved in New Age, why AA Doesn't work, why it does, why alcoholism is a disease and why it isn't, etc. But you asked me to read it and I waded through it, or rather slogged through it. There has been a lot written about how to cope, abstain, cut down, etc., but from the beginning I had no interest in any of that. It seemed very clear to me throughout the article that the secular has no clue what the problem or the answer is for addiction. I realized even while I struggled that Scripture said that because of the finished work of Christ, freedom was our birthright. Galatians 5:1, John 8:32, 36, and Romans 6 clearly say that. There is a ton of good advice out there as this guy is giving out, but all it can do is help you cope; it cannot set anyone free from their addiction. Why is this good advice relatively meaningless? Because there is no life in it. It depends on the person and what they should do and if it depends on us, it will result in failure and we usually end up worse than at the outset. As Christians we should understand that freedom is only available through the finished work of Christ. We need LIFE, and that is only available in and through Christ. But every person who has received Christ has that LIFE! That is primarily what Jesus came to give us. "I have come that they may have life and have it to the full" (John 10:10b). And if we have Christ, we have it all. If Christ is your Life and He is living in you, what else could you possibly need? When we know that the author of life lives in us and is our life, as

1

he said in John 14:6 "I AM THE WAY, THE TRUTH AND THE LIFE", that is when we begin to live free. An enormous part of freedom from addiction is understanding grace and knowing that there is nothing to do but believe and receive all that He has for you. Sin will have no dominion over you since you are not under law, but under grace (Romans. 6:14).

How did it (your freedom) happen for you?

It clicked for me in 1988 from Gillham's teaching on Romans 6 — who I was in Christ and that I was dead to sin and freed from it. My wife had kicked me out of the house and I was driving from Birmingham, AL to Lookout Mountain, TN to stay with some friends for a few days. I was driving along listening to Bill Gillham teach on Romans 6. Gillham quoted Romans 6:1, "we died to sin; how can we live in it any longer?" He said, "I know you don't feel dead to sin, you don't act dead to sin, you don't even look dead to sin. You think that is just what God says about you. You think that is just how God sees you. BUT what God says about you is the truth. How God sees you is reality. You are dead to sin whether you feel like it, act like it or look like it." That is when the lights came on for me and I knew I was free and have been for the last 32 years. Many have asked me, "What did you do"? The answer is nothing. I couldn't do anything. I was driving along in a car with a hangover. There was nothing to do as it had already been done. Jesus said, "Then you will know the truth, and the truth will set you free" (John 8:32). For the first time in my life I knew I was freed from sin and dead to it. I realized at the time that we evangelicals do what we accuse the liberals of doing. We don't feel dead to sin and our experiences do not tell us we are dead to sin so we do not believe we are. We believe what our emotions and experiences tell us instead of what

God says. "When you received the word of God, which you heard from us, you accepted it not as the word of men, but as what it really is, the word of God, which is at work in you believers" (1 Thessalonians 2:13).

But haven't you grown and matured in your freedom over the years?

I will have to admit that it has only been in the last 30 years that I have not only understood who I was in Christ, but who Christ was in me. I had understood the first part of Galatians 2:20 that I had been crucified with Christ and I no longer lived, but not the full implication of "Christ living in me". I began to understand the full implications that Christ was my life (Colossians 3:4) and that I was one Spirit with Him (1 Corinthians 6:17). I had the head knowledge, but I know now that is who I am… "Christ in me the hope of glory" (Colossians 1:27). I believe that Galatians 2:20 is the key and overriding truth that sets free. If Christ is living in me and is my life, what else could I or any Christian possibly need. What we need is to know and fully comprehend who Christ is in us, and I firmly believe that will take the rest of eternity. But I thank God that in the meantime I can live a fulfilled life of victory in peace and joy.

What do you mean that the church doesn't know what the problem and answer for addiction is?

It seems very few Christians have a clue about the problem and the answer for addiction. I include most counselors and pastors. The reason I say that is that if you look to them to get help with an addiction, most will tell you what to do. What they prescribe will be excellent things to do and most of them will be spiritual, but since "it" has already been done and "IT IS FINISHED", there is nothing left to do but believe the truth. There are countless Christians struggling with addiction (I talk to them all the time) and the bizarre thing is that they are already free. In the past 32 years, I have never seen anyone get free that didn't believe Galatians 2:20. It doesn't mean they understand the full implications of it as I did not and am not sure I do now. How can you fully comprehend that the Creator of the universe, the King of kings, the Lord of Lords lives in you? You cannot. But if they understand the old self is dead and gone, and there is nothing that they can do to shape up or improve self, and that Christ is their life, then they have taken the first step of freedom. If you don't know the old self is dead and gone, you will strive, strain and struggle to get free, do right, abstain from sin, avoid wrong, and all it accomplishes is digging a deeper hole than the one you are standing in. Most Pastors of churches will tell you to go to AA meetings and/or go to a secular treatment center. That is what my church told me to do, and I did it. Why would these churches do this? I think Neil Anderson had the answer when he said that only 10% of Christians are really free. If they don't know God's answer for addiction, then they are just giving it their best shot which means "go to AA, go to a secular treatment center, go to a psychiatrist, a psychologist, Christian counselor, secular counselor." I know as I was told all of these things to do which I dutifully did. None of them helped me because they didn't understand the problem or the solution. They did not have a clue. Of course, I did not either at the time. The answer for the issue is really very simple. The problem is spiritual bondage as it is at the core of who you are and the answer is to know and believe who you are in Christ. But when you believe who you are in Christ, you will understand it is the most liberating, earth shaking, mind-bending truth in the universe. Think about it for a minute. The Creator of the universe, the Lord of Lords, the King of Kings, lives in you and is living your life as you. You will never get over it.

Why do you say that most pastors and counselors don't understand what the answer for addiction is?

Many counselors know that what we believe about ourselves determines our actions, whether it is alcoholism, sex addiction, homosexuality, perfectionism, workaholism or codependency. And I believe we have learned that knowing who we are in Christ is the answer, but I wonder if very many of us know that Christ is living our life and it's the only life we got. It's difficult to believe the truth when everything in this world testifies against it, from our feelings, circumstances, experiences and what others say including friends, family, pastors, counselors and authors, etc. BUT IF IT IS TRUE THAT I NO LONGER LIVE BUT CHRIST IS LIVING IN ME, WHAT ELSE DO I NEED? If I really believe that truth, will I struggle with addiction or besetting sin? I don't think so. The Christians who believe they are alcoholics or even recovering alcoholics obviously do not believe 1 Corinthians 6:9-11, "Do not be deceived: Neither the sexually immoral nor idolaters nor adulterers nor male prostitutes nor homosexual offenders nor thieves nor the greedy nor drunkards nor slanderers nor swindlers will inherit the kingdom of God. And that is what some of you were. But you were washed, you were sanctified, you were justified in the name of the Lord Jesus Christ and by the Spirit of our God." Yes, that is what we were, but something radical happened. If we can just understand and believe what the finished work of Christ has accomplished, we will know that we are washed from all our sin, sanctified and set apart for God, and justified and made righteous. We are as free as we will ever be. Yes, as we believe this truth, we will begin to experience it more. There is, however, nothing for us to do but believe it. IT IS FINISHED! It has been done!

Don't you think AA, 12-Step programs, secular treatment, and Christian treatment can help in the process to get free?

I'm sure this can help some people cope, maybe get their drinking and/or drugging under control (temporarily), but so what? God has something so much better for us - freedom! My church's discipline committee sent me to a secular treatment center, and in hindsight I think it was "spiritual malpractice", but God used it in my life to bring me to the end of myself, even though it was four years later. God is not limited and can reach us no matter where we are or what we are doing. My problem with AA is that they do not believe a person will ever find freedom through AA. They believe that addiction is a disease and you will have to cope with it for the rest of your life. I have heard of people who were drinking in a bar and God clearly spoke to them. When you get down to the bottom line basics, what really matters is our personal relationship with God. The truth is that when we really understand who God is in us and that Christ is our life and is living our life in us (Galatians 2:20), we are very close, if not already there, to experiencing our freedom in Christ. EVERYTHING revolves around that incredible, life-changing and liberating truth. I know that it is very difficult for us to believe that we possess freedom in Christ, BUT we have to know and believe that truth before we experience freedom in Christ. I am convinced that the reason most have trouble believing is that our emotions (feelings) and actions (behavior) usually tell us the opposite. A poignant fact of life is that they do not tell us the truth.

7

If we are really free, shouldn't we be able to drink alcohol in moderation?

Absolutely. If people ask me when did I stop drinking, I have to reply I never did. Well, I did stop for the first year or so, but then I wondered, "If I'm not an alcoholic, but Christ is my life and I am dead to sin and freed from it, why can't I have a beer or a glass of wine when I desire"? So, if someone asks me "how long have you been sober?", I can truthfully say 32 years. What most people don't understand is that the alcoholic drinks for a different reason than most do. Most people drink to relax or for social reasons, etc., but the alcoholic does it to alter his mood, to overcome his self-consciousness, and/or medicate his emotional pain, etc. He is not comfortable in his own skin (he may be a Christian, but doesn't know who he is in Christ). Believe me, I know. I was a Christian for 18 years before I knew who I was in Christ. I do have a beer or a glass of wine now and then. It has not been a problem for the last 32 years. And the overriding reason is I know that Christ is my life, and He is living it, and I am dead to sin and freed from it. But I honestly can't imagine getting drunk and being out of control and all the crap that goes with that. That is absolutely the last thing I want to do. But the disclaimer is that "if the person doesn't know who he is in Christ, it will probably be disastrous if they ingest alcohol." So, I am not encouraging people to drink.

8

What about AA?

When I struggled with alcoholism for eight years, I attended hundreds of AA meetings. I also did quite a bit of research on it. I've read books on the history of AA and the 12 Steps. I've read a biography on Bill Wilson (co-founder of AA) who became involved in the New Age, etc. I must admit that I had somewhat of a bias against AA because it didn't offer a real answer for addiction, only how to cope with it and stop drinking by following the 12 Steps. The reason for my bias? As I read and studied the Bible (I was not a scholar, but a student), it seemed clear to me that God had an answer and it was freedom in Christ, but I didn't find it for eight years. But when I finally understood and knew the truth (John 8:32) that I had been crucified with Christ and no longer lived, but Christ lived in me, and I now lived by faith in Him (Galatians 2:20), and that I was dead to sin and freed from it (Romans 6:6, 7), and Christ was my life (Colossians 3:4)…I was free indeed (John 8:36). I believe that AA has done a better job of addressing the problem of addiction than the church. You can find an AA meeting practically anywhere in the world, but you will be hard pressed to find a church that is dealing with the issue and telling people who they are and what they have in Christ. I think AA is the world's best "answer" for addiction, although they really don't have an answer, but they do provide you with the steps to cope with the problem. If a person works the steps, I believe it will improve the quality of their life. AA does not provide freedom from addiction. Freedom is only found through the Person and finished work of Christ. I've been accused of "trashing" AA, but I do not believe I do. I just point out that a person will not find freedom through AA and the 12 Steps. I never recommend attending or not attending AA, that decision is up to the person. If asked my opinion, I tell them what I am saying here. In the final analysis, I don't believe the world and AA understand the problem and therefore certainly not the answer. I believe addiction is a spiritual problem that results in spiritual bondage. I believe every person struggling with an addiction (Christian or not) is struggling with a bad self-image and believes like I did they are insecure, inferior, inadequate and guilty, and thus an alcoholic (or addict). A believer may learn to cope and get sober for a time but will not be free in Christ (free from addiction) until they know they were crucified with Christ, dead, buried, and raised up a new creation where Christ is their life and living in them. In other words, they have to know and believe who they are in Christ and what they have in Christ to experience their freedom in Christ.

What is the church (the evangelical community) missing?

It seems that every evangelical message these days is about Jesus being with us, for us, never leaving or forsaking us. Much is said about what He has done and will do for us, but something seems to be missing. It seems in the vast majority of these messages there is a separation between Jesus and the Christian. Most of these messages are very encouraging and uplifting, but something seems to be missing. What seems to be missing is "Christ in you the hope of glory". Now I know that any true Christian worth his salt knows the truth of that, but it seems to be sadly lacking in how we live life, deal with issues and problems, and respond to Him who loved us and gave Himself for us. Do we know and believe that we were crucified with Him and we no longer live, but Christ lives in us, and the life we live we live by the faith of the Son of God who loved us and gave Himself for us (Galatians 2:20)? Do we know that Christ is our life (Colossians 3:4) and the only life we have? Do we know that we are dead to sin and freed from it (Romans 6:6, 7). Do we know that we are one Spirit with Him (1 Corinthians 6:17)? When a person believes these truths, they will experience their freedom in Christ. Didn't Jesus pray in John 17 that we would be one with Him and the Father? I believe that prayer was answered. I know that it's hard to get your mind around that. In fact, it is impossible. But we don't live by sight, but by faith (1 Corinthians 4:7). As Proverbs 3:5, 6 says, we can't understand that or figure it out. As it reads in the Message, "Trust GOD from the bottom of your heart; don't try to figure out everything on your own." (Proverbs 3:5 MSG). When you figure out things on your own, you might come up with a well-reasoned theology, but it will not do you much good. After three years of studying theology at seminary and serving in the pastorate, and eighteen years as a Christian, I was an alcoholic and a falling down drunk. I had to change my theology to experience my freedom in Christ. Or a better way to put it, I had to believe Galatians 2:20. When I believed that I was "dead to sin and freed from it", I was free. I didn't do a thing to get free. I had a hangover the day I believed the truth that I was no longer living, but Christ was living in me and I have never gotten over it. How could you get over it? It staggers the imagination. It blows your mind. You don't grasp it with your mind. As Romans 10:6 says, "If you confess with your mouth that Jesus is Lord and believe in your heart that God raised him from the dead, you will be saved." (Romans 10:9 ESV). We do not believe with our minds but with our hearts. That is who you are at the core of your being (in your heart). Heart is spirit. Stop trying to figure it out and as Jesus responded to Jairus when they told him his daughter was dead, "Ignoring what they said, Jesus told the synagogue ruler, "Don't be afraid; just believe." (Mark 5:36 NIV). Ignore the facts, the circumstances, your feelings, what others say and believe Jesus (The TRUTH). He is the way, the truth and the life (John 14:6). There is no other way; there is no other truth and there is no other life. EVERYONE who believes there is another way is living a lie. As Madame Guyon has said in her writings "Jesus is the truth and everything else is a lie." Chew on that for a while. I believe a large part of what she meant was that all who are trying to find their identity, purpose and reason for being in what this world offers are going to be sadly and tragically mistaken.

I have been diagnosed as bipolar. Does that mean I have to live with it the rest of my life?

I do not believe that bipolar is a disease and you have to live with it for the rest of your life. I do believe that there can be a genetic predisposition to bipolar, depression and addiction, but that doesn't make it a disease. Even if it is a disease that disease is in our body and our flesh and is not who we are. We are not physical beings who have received a spirit. We are spiritual beings who live in a body. When we know and believe that we no longer live but Christ lives in us and we now live by faith (Galatians 2:20); that we are not physical beings who have received a spirit but spiritual beings who live in a body, that is when we experience the freedom that has already been provided for us in Christ. As Jesus told Martha at the grave of Lazarus, "I am the resurrection and the life. He who believes in me will live, even though he dies" (John 11:25). When we know that we are one Spirit with Christ (1 Corinthians 6:17), and are dead to sin and freed from it (Romans 6:6, 7) and Christ is our life (Col. 3:4), that is when we walk free and begin to live free (Galatians 5:1, John 8:32, 36). It is the only way I have seen anyone get free, and I have seen many who have in the 32 years I have been doing this ministry. I hope you will receive this as encouraging news. I can certainly relate to you as I lived in a nightmare of hell for eight years. I'm not suggesting that you stop taking medications as prescribed by your doctor. I believe they can be helpful. What I am saying is that you are free and will experience freedom from addiction when you know and believe who you are in Christ. It doesn't happen overnight necessarily, but it is true. And generally speaking, when we come to the end of self and our resources is when we are in a position to believe the truth.

11

What do you mean when you say we must come to brokenness before we can believe the truth that sets free?

The Apostle Paul said it best, "we were under great pressure, far beyond our ability to endure, so that we despaired even of life. Indeed, in our hearts we felt the sentence of death. But this happened that we might not rely on ourselves but on God, who raises the dead" (2 Corinthians 1:9, 10). We have to be totally convinced that apart from Christ we can do nothing (John 15:5). Because until we are, we will try to live life in our strength and wisdom. We will try to get free, sanctified, mature, grow, avoid sin, and live the Christian life, all of which is pure legalism and leads to further bondage. Until we stop relying on ourselves, we will not rely on God who raises the dead. We cannot live two lives, our life and Christ's life. There is only one Christian life, and that is the life of Christ, but that life is in us and it's the only life we have. Brokenness does not come quickly or easily. It usually comes after much pain and suffering and even trauma and tragedy. But if it brings us to the point that we finally give up on ourselves and rely on God who raises the dead, it is worth it. Neil Anderson said it was the best day of his life and the birth of Freedom in Christ Ministries. Mike Harden, the founder of No Longer Bound, a Christian treatment center said, "I wouldn't take a million dollars for my brokenness, but you couldn't give me two million to go through it again". That puts it in the proper perspective. I heartily agree with both those men. I thank God and I praise Him for my brokenness as I would not be free today without it. I probably would not have a marriage and I certainly wouldn't have the ministry that I have. I often say that if it were not for my brokenness and the grace of God, I would be in prison, institutionalized, dead or worse, still in my addiction and that is not an exaggeration.

12

Do you think the problem with Christians struggling with an addictive behavior is that they are not born again?

I do not think the problem is that they are not born again. Neil Anderson has said that 90% of Christians are not experiencing their freedom because they are believing a lie. I am a prime example as I had been a Christian for 18 years and was a seminary graduate and a former pastor who was struggling with addiction. I have talked to hundreds of Christians who are struggling with addictions in the 32 years I have been free from my addiction. I don't think they would have been talking to me if they were not born again. I don't think you would ask if you were not born again. We need to realize that Satan is the ruler of this world and is the father of lies and that is really his only weapon against the Christian, but he uses it effectively to keep many Christians in bondage to addiction. I believe that when a Christian is operating in the flesh, he will look and act like an unbeliever. It is interesting that during my years of alcoholism I never doubted I was a Christian. I just thought I was one of the worst ones and God was probably sorry he saved me. My wife, my pastor, my best friend and everyone else doubted I was a Christian.

13

How do you explain the fact that Brennan Manning the famous Catholic priest, and noted author never got totally free of his addiction to alcoholism and died from complications of it?

I believe that Brennan Manning understood and portrayed the grace of God like no one else. He introduced me to the grace of God that led to my freedom from addiction. At the time I had been a Christian for 18 years and was in full-time ministry and had been struggling with alcoholism for eight years. I was reading a Wittenberg Door, a very off-center publication that always pushed the envelope. In it there was an interview with this Catholic priest (Manning). Manning said, "The only lasting freedom from self-consciousness comes from a profound awareness that God loves me as I am and not as I should be, that He loves me beyond worthiness and unworthiness, beyond fidelity and infidelity, that he loves me in the morning rain and evening rain, without caution, regret, boundary, limit or breaking point; that no matter what I do He can't stop loving me." Wow! It blew me away. I didn't know that. The seminary I attended and the denomination that ordained me taught that I was in a new covenant, but it wasn't exactly a new one rather the old covenant made better. So, there was no clear distinction between law and grace. And there was a monumental problem about your identity. They basically taught that you were a dirty rotten sinner. But Manning's words rang true to me, and I believed it. I believed that I was dead to the law, redeemed from the law and not under law, but under grace (Romans 6:14). For the next three months, I read everything I could on grace and listened to tapes (this was 33 years ago) on the grace of God, but I still wasn't free from addiction. I understood, believed and knew I was dead to the law, the very definition of grace. Grace totally frees us from condemnation (Romans 8:1), trying to please God, get our act together, improve, stop sinning, avoiding wrong, doing right, getting free, sanctified, etc. But it was not enough to free me from alcoholism. Why? What does it take? To experience freedom in Christ, you absolutely must believe and know two things. (1) You must know you are dead to the law (grace) and (2) that you are dead to sin and freed from it (identity). I had several conversations with Manning and I do not believe he knew who he was in Christ and that he was dead to sin and freed from it. At that time I understood grace but didn't know who I was in Christ, that Christ was my life (Colossians 3:4) and that I was one with Him (1 Corinthians 6:17). But one day after my wife had kicked me out of the house and I was driving out of town and listening to some tapes by Bill Gillham on Romans 6, I heard and believed the truth that I was dead to sin and freed from it, and was freed from my alcoholism 32 years ago. My life was totally and radically changed and I have spent most my time in ministry telling others this truth.

When listening to the webinars, my wife and I heard people ask this same type of questions time and again. Perhaps it's because people struggle with the concept of grace by faith. Perhaps you can begin to share what people can do to build their faith so they can better understand how much God loves them. And I'm not talking about works. I'm talking about the bi-product of faith practiced anytime you are interested in building a relationship. In other words, not all doing/living is "works."

If I knew how to tell people to build their faith, I would gladly do it. In fact, I would shout it from the rooftops. However, I have something much better to tell them. What I have to tell them is that their faith is complete and perfect. How could that be? Now that Christ lives in them (Galatians 2:20) and is their life (Colossians 3:4) and they are one spirit with Him (1 Corinthians 6:17), there is no need to try to do something to build their faith, but simply believe the truth that their faith is perfect and complete. You are certainly correct in that people struggle with the concept of grace by faith, but there is nothing for them to do. In fact, that is the problem! The more that we struggle to build our faith, get better, stop sinning, etc., the deeper the hole we dig for ourselves. When the disciples came and asked Jesus,

"What must we do to do the works God requires?" "Jesus answered, "The work of God is this: to believe in the one he has sent." (John 6:28, 29 NIV). I am sure there are countless books written about how to build faith, and the Christian bookstores are full of them. I have read many of them. But that is the problem. Paul asks, "You foolish Galatians! Who has bewitched you? Before your very eyes Jesus Christ was clearly portrayed as crucified. I would like to learn just one thing from you: Did you receive the Spirit by observing the law, or by believing what you heard? Are you so foolish? After beginning with the Spirit, are you now trying to attain your goal by human effort?" (Galatians 3:1-3). When will we believe that it is finished (John 19:30), that it has been done, and we have it all? The mystery is revealed, "To them God has chosen to make known among the Gentiles the glorious riches of this mystery, which is Christ in you, the hope of glory." (Colossians 1:27 NIV). What do we need to do? We need to believe the truth! It's that simple. It is simple, but not easy, as almost everything in this world testifies that it is not true. Almost all of our experiences and emotions, most of our friends, family, pastors, and counselors tell us it is not true. When the people came from Jairus, the synagogue ruler's house and told him, ""Your daughter is dead," they said. "Why bother the teacher anymore?"" But that was NOT the end of the story. Jesus said to Jairus, "Don't be afraid; just believe, and she will be healed." (Luke 8:51). You probably know the end of the story as Jesus came and raised her up. Most counselors and pastors know that what we believe determines our behavior, but do not seem to know the connection between that and addiction. I do not feel that Christ is my life and I am dead to sin and freed from it, but so what? IT IS THE TRUTH! Don't be afraid; just believe!!

I am currently in recovery for an addiction and it really

bothers me to hear the leader of an on-line ministry that I'm a part of continue to refer to herself and others, years after recovery, still as addicts, and also subscribes to the idea of "once an addict always an addict". I find it self-defeating and discouraging to hear the gospel and Christ's work on the cross negated in this way, as though what Christ did isn't enough. I'd like to hear your thoughts on this.

I completely agree with you. It is not only discouraging for a Christian to call themselves an addict, it's a total falsehood and a lie from the pit of hell. How can a person who has received Christ and Christ is now their life (Colossians 3:4), who is dead to sin and freed from it (Rom. 6:6, 7), who no longer lives but Christ lives in them (Galatians 2:20), and who is righteous (2 Corinthians 5 :21) be an addict? It borders on heresy and says that the finished work of Christ is not enough to set us free. I would disagree that it takes a lot of hard work to experience freedom. What it takes is to come to the end of self (brokenness) and believe the truth that sets free (John 8:32), and when we believe it as stated above we are free indeed (John 8:36). The church, by and large, has bought the lie that what Christ did is not enough, and now it is up to us. In our book, Helping Others Overcome Addictions, the first chapter is "The Lie the Church Believes About Addiction and how it keeps so many from finding freedom in Christ".

What part does the demonic play in addiction?

I agree that demons are involved in addiction, but I think you are talking about a "power encounter" where you would cast out demons, and that does not fit into what we are talking about. You said you were involved with Steps to Freedom in Christ for years, and if you read "The Bondage

Breaker" by Neil Anderson, you know that it was a ground-breaking book on demonic deliverance. The entire premise of the book is that demonic deliverance is not a "power encounter" but a "truth encounter". The primary purpose of the Steps to Freedom in Christ is to lead the person to the truth of who they are in Christ and what they have in Christ. When they believe the truth that "they no longer live but Christ lives in them", and He is their life (Col. 3:4), and they are one Spirit with Him (1 Cor. 6:17), and they are seated with him in the heavenly places "far above all rule and authority, power and dominion, and every title that can be given, not only in the present age but also in the one to come. And God placed all things under his feet" (Eph. 1:21–22 NIV), then they know that Satan has absolutely no power over them and he is a defeated enemy (Col 2:14, 15). The only weapon Satan has against the Christian is deception. Of course, you are correct in that he continually lies to us about who we are and what we have, and that the majority of Christians believe his lies and are not experiencing the freedom that Christ has been provided for them (Gal. 5:1). How do I know this? From personal experience and observation as well as clear statements of scripture. I was with Freedom in Christ Ministries for 12 years and took many through the Steps to Freedom in Christ. There were quite a few who were demonized (influenced and controlled by demons) and all who believed the truth of who they were in Christ and what they had in Christ through His finished work were set free from the demonic. Jesus said, "Then you will know the truth, and the truth will set you free." They answered him, "We are Abraham's descendants and have never been slaves of anyone. How can you say that we shall be set free? Jesus replied, "I tell you the truth, everyone who sins is a slave to sin. Now a slave has no permanent place in the family, but a son belongs to it forever. So, if the Son sets you free, you will be free indeed." (John 8:32–36 NIV). It is so clear and simple and basic in Scripture, but most Christians are not experiencing their freedom in Christ because everything else in the world, the flesh and the devil is lying to them and they believe the lies. Once a person believes the truth of Galatians 2:20 BBE that "I have been put to death on the cross with Christ; still I am living; no longer I, but Christ is living in me; and that life which I now am living in the flesh I am living by faith, the faith of the Son of God, who in love for me, gave himself up for me", they will begin to experience and live in the freedom that is theirs in Christ. I know as that is what I believed 32 years ago when I found freedom from my addiction.

What about casting out demons through a power encounter?

I am not saying that a "power encounter" will not work. What I am saying is that unless a person knows the truth of who they are in Christ and what they have in Christ, there is nothing to prevent the demon from coming back. The "truth encounter" is the Biblical way of deliverance. The truth that a Christian is seated with Christ in the heavenly places, is dead to sin and freed from sin and Christ is their life and they are one spirit with Him is the "truth that sets free" and what every Christian needs to know. Sadly, most of them don't know it and are not experiencing freedom in Christ. A third of Jesus' ministry was deliverance, BUT that was before the cross and His finished work. Now every Christian is crucified, dead, buried and raised up as a new creation and they no longer live, but Christ is living in them. The only weapon Satan has against us is deception. Of course, he is the Liar of all liars and is very good at it and keeps many from experiencing their freedom in Christ. We have it all! We have Christ in us living our lives. There is nothing more to get. When we received Christ, He came into us and is our life. When we believe this Satan loses any hold he might have on us and is forced to flee and we are free.

Isn't it a sin to drink wine (or have a beer or two)?

You say you are tormented because you still drink wine, but Scripture is very clear that drinking alcohol is not a sin, but drunkenness is a sin (Eph. 5:18). Jesus' enemies called him a drunkard because he drank wine and He also turned water into wine (John 2:9), so drinking wine could not be a sin. From what you write it seems to me that you do not understand grace but have put yourself under law trying to measure up, do right, and avoid sin. You do not seem to understand that your old self that you still seem to be trying to shape up was crucified with Christ and no longer lives, but Christ lives in you (Gal. 2:20), that Christ is your life (Col. 3:4) and you are one spirit with Him (1 Cor. 6:17) and that you are dead to sin and freed from it (Rom. 6:6, 7). Of course, you will never feel like it (at least not for long), and your circumstances will not look like it and you won't always act like it, BUT it is the truth. I loved Tullian Tchividjian's book Jesus + Nothing = Everything, but I do not think he emphasizes who you are in Christ and who Christ is in you and that is the TRUTH that sets you free. He does do a very good job of explaining grace, BUT besides understanding grace that you are dead to the law you also must know who you are in Christ, and that you are "dead to sin and freed from it" and Christ is your life and is living it in you and you are one spirit with Him. Knowing and believing who you are in Christ is the key to unlock the door to freedom from addiction.

Do we have an evil heart or a good heart after we receive Christ?

Excellent question! And if you know the correct answer, you will experience your freedom in Christ. Unfortunately, many (probably most) Christians believe they have an evil heart. As Jer. 17:9 says, "The heart is deceitful above all things, and desperately sick". But that is an old covenant reality and we are under a new covenant. We have a new heart as Ezekiel 36:26 says, "I will give you a new heart and put a new spirit in you". We will never experience our freedom until we understand we are under a new covenant. Why? Because you will not understand grace and that you are dead to the law and will try to do right, avoid sin and get free. Second, because you will not understand who you are until you understand and know you are under a new covenant. You absolutely must know that the old sinner self you were was crucified with Christ, and you no longer live, and that Christ lives in you and you now live by faith (Gal. 2:20). That old sinner self that had an addiction is dead and gone and no more. When you understand that you are under a new covenant and that you have a new heart and you are the righteousness of God in Christ (2 Cor. 5:21) is when you live free. Hebrews 8 spells it out: "This is the covenant I will make with the house of Israel after that time, declares the Lord. I will put my laws in their minds and write them on their hearts. I will be their God, and they will be my people. No longer will a man teach his neighbor, or a man his brother, saying, 'Know the Lord,' because they will all know me, from the least of them to the greatest. For I will forgive their wickedness and will remember their sins no more." By calling this covenant "new," he has made the first one obsolete; and what is obsolete and aging will soon disappear." (Heb. 8:10–13). Do not put yourself under the old covenant, which is obsolete, deciding what you are going to do to stop sinning, etc. Most Christians are trying to do the right things but cannot do what they want as the law stirs up sinful passions of the flesh For while we were living in the flesh, our sinful passions, aroused by the law, were at work in our members to bear fruit for death (Rom.7:5). We put ourselves under law when we decide what we are going to do to stop sinning, do right and avoid wrong. The operative word is "we" decide. As Christ said, "apart from me you can do nothing (John 15:5), but it seems that the only way we get to that point is via pain and suffering. But it is all worth it, as when we get there we are finally able to rely on God who raises the dead.

Is this sin ("using" on a daily basis) what's keeping me from drawing close to Jesus? Do I need to obey his commandments more so to feel his presence?

No, you don't need to obey His commandments more to feel His presence. There can be no obedience without faith. Faith comes first before obedience "through whom we have received grace and apostleship to bring about the obedience of faith for the sake of his name among all the nations" (Rom. 1:5). You just need to believe the truth that you are dead to sin and freed from it. You actually said "feel" 4 times in your message. That is a large part of the problem and why most Christians do not experience peace, freedom and joy. You will NEVER EVER feel the Holy Spirit or Christ in you as your life. Maybe now and then, but it will not last. We live by faith, not by feelings or sight. We believe the truth in our heart, and that is done by the Spirit. I do not often feel His peace and that I'm a new creation who is dead to sin and freed from it. But I believe and know that I am, and that is what makes all the difference. Don't ask me how to do that as I don't have an answer. There is no "how to". It is the truth whether we feel like it, act like it, look like it or what anyone says. The Apostle Paul put it like this: And we also thank God continually because, when you received the word of God, which you heard from us, you accepted it not as the word of men, but as it actually is, the word of God, which is at work in you who believe. (1 Thess. 2:13). Realize, however, that until you are convinced that apart from Christ you can do nothing, you will not give up on self and trust in Christ as your life.

21

How do I appropriate Christ as life that I know and believe I have?

If you know and believe you have it, then you have appropriated it. It seems to me that you are still trying to get those feelings back that have evaporated. But even if you get them back, they will evaporate again. You are trying to get the "feeling" back by reading all the books, going to the workshops, seminars, and having the workbooks, tapes, CD's, DVDs, etc. Actually, all that you are doing to appropriate Christ as life is testifying that you do not believe you do. You say you know you have the LIFE, but you don't have the joy or the peace. But you do have the joy and the peace as He (Jesus, the life) lives in you, and that is the only joy and peace available to anyone. Why don't you just start thanking God that Christ is your life and He is living in you and you are dead to sin and freed from it and He is your life and you are one Spirit with Him no matter what you feel, think or act like? You say that the next time you come to the end of yourself and the feelings are not there, how do you keep going without discouragement? It is simply not possible to live a life without discouragement. Everyone has feelings of discouragement, but they are just feelings. If you let your feelings define who you are and determine your actions you will live in defeat and bondage. You say that for two weeks all insecurity was gone; all self-consciousness was gone and all fear and feelings of inferiority was gone. But of course, it didn't last as they were just feelings. They didn't tell you the truth of who you are. Hardly a day passes that I don't have feelings of insecurity, fear, self-consciousness, and inferiority. But I remind myself they are just feelings and not the truth of who I am in Christ, and I do not have to let them define who I am and determine my actions. You are not going to get to a point where you won't have those feelings. You live in a body of flesh in a fallen world that Satan rules. Those feelings come from your flesh which is always going to be there until you go to be with Jesus. But they are just flesh patterns that developed over the years as you met your basic needs for love and acceptance apart from Christ. One last thing is you say "is not revelation something that God gives you when He gets good and ready no matter what truth you know, believe and appropriate by faith". I would say a resounding NO to that as what truth you know, believe and appropriate by faith is the truth you will experience. As for God illuminating your mind, He has already done that as you have the mind of Christ (1 Cor. 2:16). If you want to pray for revelation, I would suggest Eph. 1:17-23 "that the God of our Lord Jesus Christ, the Father of glory, may give you the Spirit of wisdom and of revelation in the knowledge of him, having the eyes of your hearts enlightened, that you may know what is the hope to which he has called you, what are the riches of his glorious inheritance in the saints, and what is the immeasurable greatness of his power toward us who believe, according to the working of his great might that he worked in Christ when he raised him from the dead and seated him at his right hand in the heavenly places, far above all rule and authority and power and dominion, and above every name that is named, not only in this age but also in the one to come. And he put all things under his feet and gave him as head over all things to the church, which is his body, the fullness of him who fills all in all." In fact, you no longer live, but Christ lives in you. When we believe that is when we begin to experience the truth that sets free, but not free of feelings of discouragement.

How can I figure out how to be free?

You said you didn't think it is "addiction so much as compulsion and turning to other things to satisfy". Actually, that is a good description of addiction. You also said that "much of the Scriptures taught in Romans are hard to comprehend in my natural mind". They are impossible to comprehend with your natural mind. You can only believe God's truth that sets free with your heart by the Spirit. You said in your email below that you are "trying to figure it out how to be free". You can't figure it out! It is spiritual truth and you only know that by faith. Rom. 10:8-10 puts it like this: "But what does it say? 'The word is near you; it is in your mouth and in your heart,' that is, the word of faith we are proclaiming: That if you confess with your mouth, 'Jesus is Lord,' and believe in your heart that God raised him from the dead, you will be saved. For it is with your heart that you believe and are justified, and it is with your mouth that you confess and are saved." You say that the behaviors control you physically, emotionally and spiritually and that is what addiction does. But the problem will never be overcome until the spiritual is addressed. The physical and emotional are just a very small part of it. The spiritual part is when you know and believe in your heart who you are in Christ (Gal. 2:20), that He is your life (Col. 3:4), that you are one spirit with Him (1 Cor. 6:17) and you are dead to sin and freed from it (Rom. 6:6, 7). When you believe that is when you walk free and begin to live free. There is nothing necessarily wrong in asking God for a revelation, but realize that you are asking for it to believe what is already true. I pray regularly Eph. 1:17-23 for myself and my family that He "may give you the Spirit of wisdom and revelation".

23

In your Overcomer's Covenant in Christ #1 of the Covenant you say that "such programs and groups can be very caring, and may result in abstinence from alcohol and drugs, but ultimately salvation and freedom can only come in Christ." My question is, what is the ultimate difference between abstinence vs freedom in Christ or the freedom that Jesus gives? For a food addict does that mean that person can eat a doughnut and not worry about it causing this person to binge on other foods for example? Or an alcoholic who is free by Jesus Christ, can they have one glass of beer or wine and not go off and get drunk?

You asked what is the difference between freedom and abstinence. Great question! And you posed the question, "does that mean that a person with a food addiction can eat a doughnut and not binge on other foods and a person with an alcohol addiction can have a beer or glass of wine and not go off and get drunk?". I use the term "person with an addiction" rather than "addict" as I do not believe a Christian is an addict. And therein lies the crux of the problem, and also the answer. When a person knows who they are in Christ and that they no longer live, but Christ lives in them (Gal. 2:20), and they are dead to sin and freed from it (Rom. 6:6, 7), and Christ is their life (Col. 3:4) and they are one spirit with him (1 Cor. 6:17), yes, they can eat a doughnut, or drink a beer or a glass of wine, and not go on an eating binge or get drunk. I learned the truth of Gal. 2:20 32 years ago and have been free of my addiction to alcohol ever since and I have a beer or a glass or two of wine whenever I want and it is not an issue. I keep beer and wine in the refrigerator and have gotten to the point that a month or so goes by and I do not have a beer or glass of wine. "So, Christ has truly set us free. Now make sure that you stay free and don't get tied up again in slavery to the law." (Gal. 5:1

NLT). Most programs (Christian and AA) tell you what to do and usually they are good things to do, but the problem is that it depends on you and it does not matter what you do or don't do until you believe the truth of who you are in Christ. It basically puts you under the slavery of the law and the power of sin is the law (1 Cor. 15:56) and sinful passions are aroused by the law (Rom 7:5). There is nothing to do but believe the truth (John 8:32, 36); it has been done. IT IS FINISHED!!! The problem is that as long as a person is trying to get something he already has, he is believing a lie and will remain in his addiction until he believes the truth that sets free. BUT, and this is a big problem, because if the person does not believe who he is in Christ the results will most likely be disastrous. However, if I believe that Christ is my life and is living in me, I cannot think of anything worse than abusing alcohol and going through all the crap that goes with it.

What about Celebrate Recovery?

Celebrate Recovery seems to be the church's answer for addiction. There are hundreds of churches offering the program which is very well organized, as are the principles and lessons they teach. They base the program on the Twelve Steps with changes they have made to Christianize it. They have eight recovery principles which are based on the beatitudes. The 12 Steps and biblical comparisons have bible verses and are basically spiritual activities to do. All of them are excellent things to do, but therein lies the problem. I have only attended a few of their meetings, but have read quite a bit about the program. It appears to me that they leave out the most important things for anyone to find freedom in Christ, such as (1) Identity in Christ, that is that the old sinner and addict that we were has been crucified with

Christ and we no longer live, but Christ is living in us (Gal. 2:20), and that we are dead to sin and freed from it (Rom. 6:6, 7). (2) We are under grace and dead to the law and redeemed from it (Rom. 6:14). In other words, there is nothing for us to do but believe the truth that IT IS FINISHED and we are under a new covenant. As I have said many times, I believe that if you work the 12 Steps (secular or Christian) it will improve the quality of your life and help you cope with your problem, BUT it will not set you free because Christ has already set you free. "So Christ has truly set us free. Now make sure that you stay free, and don't get tied up again in slavery to the law" (Gal 5:1 NLT). Freedom is only available through the finished work and person of Christ; He has provided it for us, it is there for the taking if we will believe it and receive it. There is nothing to do to get it as it has been given to us, and all we do to try to obtain it is simply an act of unbelief. I don't mean to be critical of anyone as I lived in unbelief for the first 18 years of my Christian life and struggled with alcoholism for eight of those years. But the day I believed that I was dead to sin and freed from it is the day that I found my freedom from addiction 32 years ago. What did I do to get free? Absolutely nothing! I had a hangover and was listening to a tape in a car and couldn't do anything. I'm not saying that a person shouldn't attend Celebrate Recovery. I am just saying the focus of their principles and lessons they teach is not the truth that sets free. They do a great job of providing fellowship and support that all of us need. They also do a good job of reaching out to the unchurched, and in doing so introducing them to Christ.

What can I do to get free and live the victorious Christian life?

The short answer is there is nothing you can do as you are

already free. I do not believe that freedom has anything to do with what we do. And that includes anything spiritual, such as praying, reading, studying, memorizing the Bible, fasting, going to church, and more. Over 500 years ago Martin Luther said, "Nothing you do helps you spiritually. Only faith in Christ and His word helps". The reason it has nothing to do with what we do is it has already been done. "It is for freedom that Christ has set us free. Stand firm, then, and do not let yourselves be burdened again by a yoke of slavery." (Gal. 5:1 NIV). The yoke of slavery Paul is talking about is the law. Any time I depend on what I do to make something happen, I put myself under the law, which is a yoke of bondage as "The sting of death is sin, and the power of sin is the law." (1 Cor. 15:56 NIV). When we decide what we will do to deal with our problems, whether it is addiction or relating to our life, we have enabled the power of sin, which is the law. Why? Simply unbelief, which is deception! We do not believe "I have been crucified with Christ and I no longer live, but Christ lives in me. The life I live in the body, I live by faith in the Son of God, who loved me and gave himself for me." (Gal 2:20 NIV). As Martin Luther said, the root of all sin is unbelief. He also said, "The law says do this and never is it done. Grace says believe in this and it is already done". I am not saying "don't pray and read your Bible" as I do it every day. I am saying do not depend on what you do to set you free because you are already free "For we know that our old self was crucified with him so that the body of sin might be done away with, that we should no longer be slaves to sin — because anyone who has died has been freed from sin." (Rom. 6:6–7 NIV). Jesus said, "Then you will know the truth, and the truth will set you free." (John 8:32 NIV). It has been done. IT IS FINISHED! Of course, this is the hardest truth in the world to believe as our feelings, circumstances and experiences tell us the opposite. As someone has said it is easier to obey the law, than believe the truth. If Christ is your life (Col. 3:4) and is living in you (Gal. 2:20) and you are one spirit with Him (1 Cor. 6:17), what else do you need?

What keeps us from living the abundant, victorious life that is ours in Christ? Satan? Well, yes, but how does he do it? What is his weapon that is so powerful? Of course it is the lie, but how many of us realize that and do anything about it as we falter, fumble and fail in life as I've spent too much of my life doing. Why is the lie so effective?

Because it is the most powerful weapon in the world next to the truth. Wars have been fought and millions have died as Hitler and Stalin got the populace to believe their lies. If Satan can get us to believe a lie about our self, God, and life, then he can control our life and make us miserable. And he does this very effectively with most Christians. No, this is not in the least an exaggeration. What percentage of Christians do you know that are living free in joy, peace and victory? I know some, but not that many. So, what do we need to live free and in victory? The truth? Well, yes, but not in the way most of us think. It is not having knowledge of the Scripture and being familiar with what the Bible says. It is not memorizing scripture, meditating on it, praying it, quoting it (in times of temptation), listening to it, reading it, thinking it, speaking it (aloud), etc. You can take my word for it. I was a seminary graduate, former pastor, an avid student of the Scriptures. I memorized chapters of the Bible, in fact the two best chapters in the Bible on freedom and victory (Romans 6 and Colossians. 3). While all this was going on I struggled with alcoholism for eight long, miserable, nightmarish years. I found my freedom 32 years ago when I learned the simple truth of Gal. 2:20, that the old self that I was had been crucified with Christ and I no longer lived, but Christ was living my life and I lived by the faith of the Son of God who loved me and gave Himself for me. I had been a Christian 18 years at that point and all the truth I knew had little effect on my experiencing the freedom in Christ that had been given to me. Yes, I needed to know the truth that I was dead to sin and freed from it. But what I needed the most was to know the reason I was dead to sin and freed from it (Rom. 6:6, 7) was because Christ was now my life (Col. 3:4) and was living it.. I needed to know the truth, but what I really needed to know was the TRUTH and that the TRUTH lived in me and was my life. Yes, I needed to know that the living embodiment of the TRUTH, Jesus Himself, was living in me. When I understood and believed that it changed everything. Yes, I still have my struggles and my ups and downs, but my struggles with addiction were over. Truthfully, I didn't know that much 32 years ago, but it was enough to get me off the road to destruction, save my life and my marriage and give me a recovery ministry. The message of my ministry has been and still is Christ is our life, our identity, and we are dead to sin and freed from it. I have coauthored five books on freedom from addiction and that has been the core message in each of them. This message of "Christ in you, the hope of glory" (Col. 1:27) is the only thing that I've seen that has helped anyone find any freedom. There are lots of ways to cope with addiction, and the 12 Steps are the best way the world has found to deal with it. But the only people I have ever seen who found real, true and lasting freedom from addiction were those who understood, knew and believed that Christ was their life. Two months before I found my freedom I heard a message by Anabel Gillham on John 14:20 when Jesus said On that day you will realize that I am in my Father, and you are in me, and I am in you that greatly impacted me, but I didn't understand it at the time. I asked God to reveal that truth to me and when He did I realized Christ was my life. In the past 32 years I believed I have grown in my understanding Christ as life in me, but it is still the basic core message. If we pause and think about it then "if I no longer live but Christ lives in me" what else could I possibly need? Over the 50 years that I have been a Christian and the 35 years I have been in full-time ministry I have known many Christians who were very knowledgeable about the Bible, but few who really understood Christ as life and were really living free. As I was listening to a praise song this morning, there was a phrase that said, "His presence silences every lie". I had heard it before, but this morning I really heard it. THAT'S IT! We can hear truth, listen to it, read it, memorize it, quote it, say it aloud, BUT when we know and believe and have a consciousness of His presence in us and know He is our life, it will stop, shatter, and obliterate the lies that we hear every day.

Yes, truth really does set us free, but understand that the Word of God is not written words in the Bible, but Jesus. In the beginning was the Word, and the Word was with God, and the Word was God (John 1:1). It is not the words of scripture that set us free, but the WORD who has come to live in us. There is no "what" that can set us free. Paul didn't say "What will set me free", but WHO. Thanks be to God through Jesus Christ our Lord! (Rom. 7:25). Jesus said, I am THE WAY, THE TRUTH, AND THE LIFE (John 14:6). Since I found my freedom I have ministered primarily to those struggling with addictive behavior. Most are looking for a way to overcome their addiction. Therein lies a major part of the problem as they are looking for what they can do. But there is nothing for them to do, as it has already been done. Many of them turn to the Scriptures as I did and study them assiduously. They all want a better life, but the only real LIFE is found in Christ and when Christians find Christ in them as their life, they find freedom.

It really is so simple, and I think that's one of the reasons so few find freedom. After all, I'm a seminary graduate and an ordained minister. I can figure it out and make it happen. I gave it my best shot for 18 years, delving into the Scriptures for the key to set me free and ended up a falling down drunk. But the key - He was in me. It is simple but not easy, as everything in this life tells us that Christ is not our life and it is up to us. When Jesus was on his way to Jairus', the synagogue ruler's house to heal his daughter who was at the point of death, some people came from Jairus' house and told him, "Don't bother the teacher any more, your daughter is dead (Mark 5:35). Ignoring what they said, Jesus told him, Don't be afraid, just believe (Mark 5:36). And He raised her from the dead (Mark 5:41, 42).

How Can I Believe the Truth that sets free?

This is the question that I get in my ministry over and over. My ministry is to teach, train, equip and provide resources that show people how to find true and lasting freedom from addictions. My message is very simple. In a nutshell, it is that "Your old self was crucified with Christ and you are dead to sin, freed from it and you no longer live, but Christ lives in you and the life you now live you are living by the faith of the Son of God who loved you and gave Himself for you" Rom. 6:6, 7; Gal. 2:20. By the way, I have noticed that when people believe that they find true and lasting freedom. I think a large part of the problem is that it is too simple. That is why I went to seminary and got educated beyond the level of my intelligence. I just hung up the phone talking with a guy who has some "intellectual" problems with "the truth that sets free." I told him that I thought that a greater education and a higher intelligence is a barrier to believing the truth that sets free. I know that my theological education and what I thought was my higher intellect was for me. I have met many people with little education who had a greater grasp of the truth than I did. We do not believe God's truth through our intellect and with our minds. We believe it with our hearts/spirit. Faith has little to do with our minds and intellect and is a big stumbling block for many. It was for me.

However, most really struggle with this truth and ask, "How can I believe the truth?". That really isn't their question. They are really asking, "How can I get a feeling or an awareness that this is true?". Of course, the answer is you cannot, or if you do, it won't last and you will be right back where you were asking the same question again. I'm not putting down anyone or accusing anyone as I have asked that question many times myself. What if on a bright, sunny day in Atlanta with the temperature hovering near 100, someone walks up to you, wipes the sweat off his brow and says, "How can I believe the truth that the sun is shining; do I need to pray longer, read my bible more, memorize scripture, get counseling, etc.?" I am confronted with that question in many forms—not about the sun shining, but believing the truth of their being dead to sin, freed from it, and their oneness with Christ.

I really believe the question almost all are asking is, "I know that is what God says, but everything else I hear and feel seems so real and it's the opposite of what God is saying. My feelings, my behavior, and what everyone else says including pastors, Christian counselors, Christian friends, etc. are saying the opposite." The answer is you will never believe if you must have visible proof, an awareness, or a feeling. Scripture is clear that it is only by faith that we receive and appropriate truth. What is faith? It is looking to, depending on, trusting in, receiving and believing, what you cannot see. It is a transaction done by the Spirit/heart and cannot be confirmed physically and materially. It is helpful to me to know that I am not a physical being who has received a Spirit, but a spiritual being who lives in a body. My body is not who I am and one of these days my body is going to give out and die, but I will live on eternally. To be absent from the body is to be present with the Lord.

Faith according to Merriam Webster is "firm belief in something for which there is no proof". I think they mean no physical proof. The bible says "Faith is the assurance of things hoped for, the conviction of things not seen". Abraham is called the "Father of Faith". He believed in God who gives life to the dead and calls into being things which do not exist (Rom. 4:17) . Whoa! There is the Key! Abraham believed God. He believed what He said and what He would do. He believed God could raise the dead and raise his son from the dead and by His word speak the creation into existence. WOW! Do you and I believe that? What you and I are called to do is to believe what He has done. IT IS FINISHED! It is a done deal that we are in Christ and He is in us and He is our life (John 14:20, Col. 3:4).

When Jesus cursed the fig tree and Peter pointed out to Him that it was withered, He said, "Have faith in God" (Mark 11:22). When Jesus was on the way to Jairus' house to heal his daughter who was dying, some people came from his home and said to Jesus, "Don't bother the teacher anymore, your daughter is dead." Ignoring what they said, Jesus said, 'Don't be afraid, just believe' To have faith in God and to believe Him you must ignore everything else. You need to ignore the circumstances, your feelings, what others say (including most Christians). We are not a society who believes in the supernatural and miracles.

When we ask that question, "How can I believe the truth", we are really making a statement of unbelief and saying we don't believe the truth that we are dead to sin and freed from it and Christ is our life, because I don't have a sign, a feeling, an awareness or any visible proof. To look for this visible proof is unbelief and as long as you look for it you will never get it. Unfortunately, that is where most Christians live. They wouldn't dare declare that, but their lives demonstrate that is what they believe. As my friend and pastor says, they live like practical atheists. But it is true whether you and I believe it or not.

We cannot get any freer than we already are (Gal. 5:1, John 8:36). We cannot get any more complete than we already are. We cannot get any more righteous than we already are. If Christ is in me and I am in Him and He is living my life, then what else do I need? Do I really need more than Christ? I have it all.

Norman Grubb tells of the time when he was confronted with the truth of Gal. 2:20 when he and his wife Pauline were in Africa as missionaries, but both of them realized it was not a reality to them. They decided to stay up one night until they could declare that it was. They did, although Norman admitted he had no feeling or awareness of it, but he was going to stand on the truth of it. He took a postcard and drew a tombstone on it and wrote "Here lies the old Norman Grubb". And it was two years later before he really understood and realized that Gal. 2:20 was a reality in his life. When I learned the truth of Gal. 2:20 32 years ago and was freed from my alcoholism, I wrote a booklet called, The Key to the Victorious Christian Life and put a tombstone on the front of it, with "Here lies the Old…Born in Adam… Died in Christ… with the verses of Gal. 2:20 and Rom. 6:6, 7. I've distributed thousands of them. Call or email me if you would like one and I will send it to you or you can buy an expanded edition on Amazon.com.

It is the truth that you are dead to sin, freed from it and the old self you were was crucified with Christ and you no longer live, but Christ lives in you and the life you live, you live by the faith of the Son of God who loved you and gave Himself for you. It is true whether you believe it, feel it, act like it, look like it or not. Truth is what God says, regardless of how you feel. What are you going to believe in—the world, America, the Constitution, Senators, Congressman, the President, the economy, the stock market, yourself - God forbid! Jesus says, "Don't be afraid, just believe"!

Hyper-Grace!?!?

Note: More details around the question. "I'm the one who asked you about hyper-grace this evening at your webinar. I have read three of your books and have been absolutely fascinated by them. I bought a book for my son who struggles with addiction and have been trying to get him to read it. I hope you were not offended that I asked the question. I have come across this term only recently. I am also a big fan of Michael Brown who is an author and writer on Charisma news. He has been speaking quite a bit about hyper-grace. From what I can read, it is becoming a big concern to me. And so I am including the definition of hyper-grace below and am hoping you can set me straight. The term hyper-grace has been used to describe a new wave of teaching that emphasizes the grace of God to the exclusion of other vital teachings such as repentance and confession of sin. Hyper-grace teachers maintain that all sin, past, present, and future, has already been forgiven, so there is no need for a believer to ever confess it. Hyper-grace teaching says that, when God looks at us, He sees only a holy and righteous people. The conclusion of hyper-grace teaching is that we are not bound by Jesus' teaching, even as we are not under the Law; that believers are not responsible for their sin; and that anyone who disagrees is a pharisaical legalist. In short, hyper-grace teachers "pervert the grace of our God into a license for immorality" (Jude 1:4) and flirt with antinomianism."

No, we do not exclude repentance and confession.

1) Repentance means to most a change of behavior, but the Greek word metanoia means to "change the mind". Of course, when you change your mind, your behavior will eventually change. When you repented and believed the gospel, you changed your mind from unbelief to belief. Likewise, when you repent with respect to your identity in Christ, you change your mind or thinking from believing you're a sinner to accepting the truth that you're a holy, loved, and righteous saint in Christ. Now, don't you think your behavior will eventually change with that type of new thinking? Our emphasis is on believing the truth; Christ in you (expressing His life through you on this earth) and you in Christ (a new creation, dead to sin and freed from it). Scripture is clear that only God grants repentance (2 Tim. 2:25) and His kindness leads to repentance (Rom. 2:4). Heb. 6:1 says that repentance and faith for salvation is an elementary teaching. If that's so, what is advanced? Faith, of course, in the finished work of Christ and knowing that we are new creations (2 Cor. 5:17), Christ is our life (Col. 3:4), and that we are one Spirit with Him (1 Cor. 3:17). And the key to everything, the ultimate and crowning glory, "I have been put to death on the cross with Christ; still I am living; no longer I, but Christ is living in me; and that life which I now am living in the flesh I am living by faith, the faith of the Son of God, who in love for me, gave himself up for me." (Galatians 2:20 BBE). WOW! Whoa! I don't know if that's hyper-grace or not, but I know that changes everything. I'm no longer living, but Christ is living in me. That's an earth shaking, mind blowing, and paradigm altering truth that when you believe it you will never, ever be the same.

2) Confession – First of all – ALL sin has already been forgiven (though it seems most don't really believe it and many Christians are weighed down by guilt, shame and condemnation). Here again scripture is clear that "There is therefore now no condemnation for those who are in Christ Jesus. For the law of the Spirit of life has set you free in

Christ Jesus from the law of sin and death." (Romans 8:1–2 ESV). And also "Blessed are those whose lawless deeds are forgiven, and whose sins are covered; blessed is the man against whom the Lord will not count his sin." (Romans 4:7–8 ESV). However, we do not exclude confession. Confess in the original language means to "agree with". I confess sin but I immediately praise, worship and thank Him that it is covered and He will never count it against me. However, for many believers, confession is a way to gain forgiveness. I have one question...how can you gain what you already have in Christ? You are already forgiven and God has chosen not to remember your sin any longer...why do we keep bringing it up, begging God for what He has already provided? Acknowledge your sin as sin, but thank God it has been taken care of at the cross (no more begging); that does NOT lessen your sin, it magnifies God's grace and the finished work at the cross. What's next, "are we to continue in sin so that grace may increase? May it never be! How shall we who died to sin still live in it?" Romans 6:1-2 (NASB). Go be who God made you to be, holy, righteous, and loving in Christ.

3) YES, when God looks at us He only sees holy and righteous people. How? Why? Because the old sin-loving sinner we used to be was crucified, dead, buried and no more (Gal. 2:20) and Christ is our life (Col. 3:4). Jesus prayed "that they may all be one, just as you, Father, are in me, and I in you, that they also may be in us, so that the world may believe that you have sent me" (John 17:21 ESV). Do you think the Father answered Jesus' prayer? "And by that will, we have been made holy through the sacrifice of the body of Jesus Christ once for all"..."because by one sacrifice he has made perfect forever those who are being made holy." (Hebrews 10:10, 14 NIV). And who are those being made holy? Each person who places their faith in the death, burial and resurrection of our Lord Jesus Christ for forgiveness and life.

4) The truth is we are not bound by Jesus' teaching, the Ten Commandments or any law. Scripture is clear that "likewise, my brothers, you also have died to the law through the body of Christ, so that you may belong to another, to him who has been raised from the dead, in order that we may bear fruit for God. For while we were living in the flesh, our sinful passions, aroused by the law, were at work in our members to bear fruit for death. But now we are released from the law, having died to that which held us captive, so that we serve in the new way of the Spirit and not in the old way of the written code" (Rom. 7:4, 6 ESV). The law, of course, is still in effect, and there is nothing wrong with it. "Now we know that the law is good, if one uses it lawfully, understanding this, that the law is not laid down for the just but for the lawless and disobedient, for the ungodly and sinners, for the unholy and profane," (1 Timothy 1:8–9 ESV). The problem is that we cannot keep the Law and Paul tells us it is no longer for those who are in Christ, "For Christ is the end of the law for righteousness to everyone who believes." (Romans 10:4 ESV). Christ fulfilled the righteous requirement of the Law and we are in Him and He is in us! The Law has been satisfied in Christ "in order that the righteous requirement of the law might be fulfilled in us, who walk not according to the flesh but according to the Spirit." (Romans 8:4 ESV). We don't flirt with antinomianism, which means "no law", we know that we are dead to sin and freed from it; Christ is our life, and the believer who understands his or her new identity will behave morally as they trust Christ as their life. There is really only one law for the believer. Jesus said, A new commandment I give to you, that you love one another, even as I have loved you, that you also love one another. (John 13:34) and the Apostle John reiterated it, not as though [I were] writing to you a new commandment, but the one which we have had from the beginning, that we love one another. (2 John 5). In fact God expects the believer, and enables them through Christ, to behave much better than

just keeping the Law, we are designed and equipped to be holy and love as Christ loved.

5) We don't pervert the grace of God into a license for immorality. In fact, the opposite is true. The only way I've ever seen anyone find freedom from any bondage and/or addictive behavior is when he or she understood "for sin will have no dominion over you, since you are not under law but under grace." (Romans 6:14 ESV). I struggled with alcoholism for eight years and found my freedom over 32 years ago when I understood the grace of God and that He had already done everything through His finished work of the cross. When I finally understood Gal. 2:20 after 18 years as a Christian I was "free indeed". I have now been free for 32 years! Hallelujah! Praise God!! May His Name be praised throughout all eternity!!!

If a person is an alcoholic, then he must not be a Christian. Is that not so?

"Those who continue in sin have neither seen Him or known Him" (1 John 3:6) seems to be the linchpin on which you make your case. I think you expressed your opinion that "the person must not be saved if he is an alcoholic". That to me presents a major problem as I do not think I am able to know whether a person is saved or not. That is definitely above my pay grade. That is a judgment I believe only God can make. I don't want to go into too much detail on my testimony on how I was freed from my alcoholism, but I struggled with it for eight long miserable years before I experienced my freedom 32 years ago. My struggle began after I had been a Christian for eight years, had graduated from Seminary and served in the pastorate. Everyone doubted I was a Christian during this time, and I mean everyone including my wife, my pastor, and my two best friends. However, I NEVER doubted it. I believed I was the sorriest Christian who ever lived, and God was probably sorry that he saved me. I lived in daily torment because I was in bondage and couldn't get out of it, even though I was trying everything I knew to do and everything anyone told me. During this nightmare, which I couldn't wake up from, I sincerely and desperately wanted my life to be what God wanted it to be. I prayed daily, read scripture daily, memorized scripture, went to church regularly, but it seemed to no avail. The church of which I was a member called me before the discipline committee and sent me to a secular treatment center. They had no idea what to do with me, but tried their best to help me. It seems to me that most churches and pastors have little idea of the problem and answer to addiction. During this time, all I ever wanted was deliverance from the bondage of addiction; I just wanted to be a decent Christian and a normal husband. 32 years ago my wife had kicked me out of the house and I was driving out of town with a horrible hangover. I was listening to a tape by Bill Gillham on Romans 6 and he quoted, "What shall we say, then? Shall we go on sinning so that grace may increase? By no means! We died to sin; how can we live in it any longer?" (Romans 6:1–2 NIV). Gillham then said, "You're dead to sin. You don't act like it. You don't feel like it, you don't even look like it, but you're dead to sin". And that's when the lights came on and I knew the truth, "that we know that our old self was crucified with him so that the body of sin might be done away with, that we should no longer be slaves to sin — because anyone who has died has been freed from sin." (Romans 6:6–7 NIV). By the way, I have been free from addiction ever since, have coauthored five books on freedom from addiction, and serving in a recovery ministry that teaches freedom in Christ. Someone might ask, "How was I changed that day? What happened to me so that I was free from addiction?". The answer is that I was not changed. I had been in Christ and Christ had been in me for 18 years and I had been "dead to sin and freed from it" all those years, but I had believed the lie that my thoughts, feelings and behavior defined who I was and determined how I behaved instead of who I was (Christ in me) and what Christ had done (the finished work of Christ). Nothing changed in me except that I no longer believed the lie but believed the truth, that "Therefore, if anyone is in Christ, he is a new creation; the old has gone, the new has come!" (2 Corinthians 5:17 NIV). I believed the truth that "I have been crucified with Christ and I no longer live, but Christ lives in me. The life I live in the body, I live by faith in the Son of God, who loved me and gave himself for me." (Gal. 2:20 NIV). By the way, if you had closely observed me for those eight years you would have noticed that the alcoholic behavior of getting drunk, acting stupid and ungodly actions was only a small percentage of the time. I didn't drink every day and many days I was crying out to God, praying reading scripture, etc. The ungodly behavior was certainly enough to warrant anyone to doubt my salvation and to make my life a disaster of rack and ruin, BUT God seems to specialize in redeeming us from all that (though it does seem to take longer for some of us). However, I really don't think I would have the ministry I do today, the marriage that I have, and the freedom, peace and joy I have if I hadn't gone through it. In fact, because of that I thank God for it. It seems to me that a major problem in evangelical Christianity is that we really don't understand the full implications of the Gospel and the finished work of Christ. If we did, we would stop telling people what to do to stop their addictive, ungodly and bad behavior and tell them who they are in Christ and what He has done for them. That is what I do in my ministry. When I tell them these truths, I see lights come on and people began to believe the truth and experience the freedom that has already been provided for them in Christ. I will be the first to admit it doesn't come easily to most as they are convinced it is up to them and what they must do as that is what they hear from most Christians, churches, pastors, counselors, books, etc. I have found that a lot of our problems in helping Christians experience their freedom is that we don't start with the truth of the finished work of Christ. If we don't, then everything is askew, especially if we go to the old testament and even the new testament. If we don't start with the truth that sin has been dealt with and is no more, and Christ is our life (Col. 3:4), and we are one Spirit with Him (1 Cor. 6:17), we are just promoters of law and legalism and put people in deeper bondage (as I did in my pastorate). I John 3:9 says, "No one who is born of God practices sin, because His seed abides in him; and he cannot sin, because he is born of God". You might think that proves your case, but if we interpret that verse in the light of the finished work and what Christ has done, it is saying that a born-again believer is in Christ and Christ is in him (John 14:20) and he cannot sin. Well, what about all that sinful behavior and ungodly actions? That is NOT who we are. We cannot sin as sin has been taken care of and is no more. At the core of our being and in our heart (our spirit) we cannot sin. As you said, if Christ is in us and is our life, how can we continue to sin? If we just knew how good the Good News is and how finished the finished work of Christ was, the problem of sin and addiction would be over once and for all. It is over as Christ said on the cross, IT IS FINISHED!!! As I say, if Christ is in you and you are in Christ, what more could you possibly need? All you need is to believe the truth as Jesus said in John 8:32, "Then you will know the truth, and the truth will set you free". I know I've said a lot and I'm sure you are probably not convinced, but as I said that was not my purpose. I don't consider myself a theologian but a student of the scriptures, and I'm still learning. I don't have the time or interest to get into theological debates. I spent too much time debating the truth in seminary and my years in the pastorate (and I really didn't know the truth). My life and my ministry are based on the truth I believed 32 years ago and I spend my time sharing it with people struggling with addictive behaviors. By the way, I believe everyone has had a struggle with something that keeps them from experiencing their freedom in Christ. Not everyone is open to what I believe and teach, but many are and it keeps me busy. The ones who are open are those who have usually tried it all and have finally given up on self and come to the end of their resources.

I have never gotten to the point where I feel that Christ is my life and I am living it. I have been so strong at times and so weak at others. I just don't get it?

I can relate to everything you have written. I also have been so strong at times and so weak at others, and to be truthful I am still that way at times. I have never gotten to the point where I feel that Christ is my life and is living it, but then again that is not the point. The truth is that He is my life, and He is living it whether I feel like it or even act like it. That's the truth. By the way, you and I in our own strength, wisdom and resources will never be strong. There is nothing good in us, that is our flesh (Rom. 7:18) and all of our strength, wisdom and resources is flesh. Apart from Christ, we can do nothing (John 15:5), but we can do all things through Him. As Paul said in 2 Cor. 12:7-10, he delighted in his weaknesses, so that the power of Christ would rest on him, because when he was weak, then he was strong. You and I will never be anything but weak. We will never get our act together, improve, stop sinning, and do right. But therein is the crux of the problem, and also the answer. We will never get our act together as it was crucified on the cross and we no longer live but Christ lives in us and we now live by faith. As Martin Luther said over 500 years ago "Nothing you do helps you spiritually, only faith in Christ". Only by believing what Christ has accomplished on the cross and believing the truth will we accomplish anything. You say that you tried everything and tried to do nothing. You don't have to try to do nothing as apart from Christ nothing is all you can do. So that brings up the question, "How do I believe"? Rom. 10:5-10 says that the word of faith (truth) is in your mouth and there is nothing for you to do, but believe it and speak it, for you believe with your heart and speak it with your mouth and it is already in you. There is nothing to do. I think you are in a good place, i.e., right where God wants you. We have to get to the place where we know there is nothing that we can do and there is nothing in us (our flesh) to help us.

31

What if a person is a lesbian? Homosexual?

In answer to your question, the lesbian / homosexual issue is an addiction and identity issue. I have worked with quite a few people struggling with that issue. It really doesn't matter what the issue is that is keeping people from experiencing their freedom in Christ. When they understand who they are in Christ and what they have in Christ, they experience their freedom. It sounds simplistic, and it is simple (but not easy), but when a person understands and believes in their heart the truth of Gal. 2:20, and that Christ is their life (Col. 3:4), and they are dead to sin and freed from it (Rom. 6:6, 7), and are one Spirit with Him (1 Cor. 6:17) they are free. I remember one man who lost his marriage and family (wife and 3 children) and was kicked out of his church when he acted out on his homosexual feelings. As a teenager, he was taken in by two prominent men who brought him into a homosexual relationship. When he saw, and realized that it happened because he desperately was seeking male acceptance and affirmation and not because he was a homosexual, he exclaimed "I was duped!" Yes, he was and it was Satan the father of lies and the great deceiver who did it. He read a few of Neil Anderson's and my books and I took him through the Steps to Freedom in Christ (30 years ago); he learned and believed who he was in Christ and he is free today. No one is born gay and therefore by birth a homosexual or a lesbian. God didn't make a mistake that needs to be changed by expensive surgery. The only way anyone will find freedom, peace, joy and fulfillment in this life is in a relationship with God and knowing who they are in Christ. It doesn't come easy as we have to give-up on our life and all the carefully conceived ways we have developed to live life in our own strength and wisdom (our flesh), but when we do, we find it is the most liberating and incredible thing we can do. Keep in touch and let me know if I can help you or your ministry.

Why do you say that Gal. 2:20 is the key and when people understand and believe it is when they get free?

"I have been put to death on the cross with Christ; still I am living; no longer I, but Christ is living in me; and that life which I now am living in the flesh I am living by faith, the faith of the Son of God, who in love for me, gave himself up for me." (Gal. 2:20 BBE). The reason Gal. 2:20 is the key to being free, living free and staying free is because: (1) the self that you believe you are and you are struggling to improve and get free is no more. The old sinner self that you were that was addicted has been crucified, dead, buried, and is no more. You can stop trying to shape up the old self that you were as he (she) is dead and gone. (2) you have been raised up as a new creation, "Therefore, if anyone is in Christ, he is a new creation. The old has passed away; behold, the new has come." (2 Cor. 5:17 ESV). You do not need to do anything to make this true in your life. It is true, and when you believe it is when you will experience the truth that sets you free

(John 8:32). When you understand that Christ is your life (Col.3:4), and you are one with Him (1 Cor. 6:17), and you are dead to sin and freed from it (Rom. 6:6, 7) is when you experience the freedom that has been given to you. (3) You now live by faith, not by sight, feelings or circumstances. "We live by faith, not by sight." (2 Cor. 5:7). The reason countless Christians are in bondage to addiction is they are living by sight, feelings and circumstances. When a Christian knows the truth of what the finished work of Christ accomplished, they will live free. Why? Because they are free! There is nothing for them to do but believe the truth of what Christ accomplished on the cross and the fact that they were in Him when it happened and that they were crucified, dead, buried and raised up as new creations who are dead to sin and freed from it regardless of how they feel, what they look like or what their experiences tell them.

33

I have already watched the Fireproof Movie twice since it arrived. What stands out to me is selfishness! I have been SO selfish with my wife, especially in the area of EXPECTING her to gratify me physically. Then as I was going back to the Love Dare devotional, I realized that on the first 2 attempts, a few years ago, I was just faking it. My heart was not ALL IN. I was just going thru' it getting my checks in the boxes and not giving God and His Spirit the chance to transform me. It seemed like I needed to "camp out" a whole week on the first 2 days of Patience and Kindness. Then as I was talking to my wife last night, she told me straight out that what she was looking for in a loving husband was: Patience and Kindness. A lot of times this prideful idiot (me) needs to be hit over the head with a baseball bat to get it. And this was the Holy Spirit's gentle "baseball bat", confirming thru' my wife's direct words to focus on Patience & Kindness to develop my character.

Note: I received this email from a man that I was in contact with for a year so. As you can see from it he was very sincere but sincerely wrong in his approach. It really is not a question. He was telling me what he thought he should do and was going to do and wanted my input which I gave.

I really hope my reply doesn't offend you, but am driven to do so as I know it is only "the truth that sets free". There is so much deception in what you have written that as long as you believe it and pursue the course that you are on I believe it will lead further into bondage. (1) First of all, God doesn't need to transform you. You don't need to pray for deliverance from addiction as you have already been delivered. You are a new creation in Christ (2Cor. 5:17). You have died to sin and been freed from it (Rom. 6:6, 7). Christ is your life (Col. 3:4) and you, as wild and crazy as it sounds, are one spirit with Christ (1 Cor. 6:17). Most Christians spend their lives trying to get something they already have (righteousness - dead to sin and freed from it) and trying to be someone they already are (Christ as life). (2) I'm not trying to put you down as I lived in a nightmare from hell for eight years of my addiction to alcoholism and was beating up on myself and trying all the things that you are trying. I went through two treatment centers and 30 other things that I listed in my testimony that I tried. By the way, God used them all, primarily to bring me to a point of brokenness so I would come to the end of myself and my resources and give up on myself and look to God. I believe that was what the Apostle Paul experienced when he said, "We were under great pressure, far beyond our ability to endure, so that we despaired even of life. Indeed, in our hearts we felt the sentence of death. But this happened that we might not rely on ourselves but on God, who raises the dead" (2 Cor. 1:8–9). I believe that most of the pain, suffering and failure we go through happens so that we might not rely on ourselves but on God who raises the dead. If you are like me it takes a lot to get us there. I was 51 years old, had been a Christian for 18 years and struggling with alcoholism for 8 years when the lights came on for me and I realized there was nothing for me to do as IT IS FINISHED! By the way all of the pain, suffering and failure was worth it. I wouldn't take anything for it and I praise God and thank Him for it. I would not have the marriage, ministry and life of freedom, peace and joy without it. (3) What did I do to get free? ABSOLUTELY NOTHING! In fact I had a hangover that day and my wife Julia had kicked me out of the house and I was on my way out of town. But I believed the truth I heard Bill Gillham teaching on Romans 6 that I was dead to sin and freed from it. I was trying very diligently to die to sin and get freed from it, but when I believed what God said and didn't do anything I found my freedom from alcoholism 32 years ago and God gave me this ministry to tell others what Jesus had finished and said, "Then you will know the truth, and the truth will set you free" (John 8:32). (4) You seem to have bought the lie that you can improve yourself, get better, stop sinning, get free from addiction, avoid wrong and do right. NOT! We cannot improve ourselves because, "you died, and your life is now hidden with Christ in God" (Col. 3:3). You cannot shape up a dead man. You cannot beat a dead horse and bring him back to life. What you can do is realize that your old self was crucified with Christ and Christ lives in you (Gal. 2:20) and live by faith in that truth. Why do so few believe this and live like this? Primarily because they have not been disabused of the lie that it is up them and that they can do what it takes. As Paul said, "You foolish Galatians! Who has bewitched you? Before your very eyes Jesus Christ was clearly portrayed as crucified. I would like to learn just one thing from you: Did you receive the Spirit by observing the law, or by believing what you heard? Are you so foolish? After beginning with the Spirit, are you now trying to attain your goal by human effort?" (Gal. 3:1-3). That is where most Christians live and what most well-meaning counselors and pastors are telling people to do. (5) I don't doubt that you have been selfish, but that is only because you don't know who you are in Christ and Who Christ is in you. If you believe you are the same old sin-loving sinner, you will act that way. If you believe you are an alcoholic, you will spend your life trying to stop drinking or getting drunk. We always act consistently with whom we perceive ourselves to be. But according to God's Word, that is NOT who you are. "Do you not know that the wicked will not inherit the kingdom of God? Do not be deceived: Neither the sexually immoral nor idolaters nor adulterers nor male prostitutes nor homosexual offenders nor thieves nor the greedy nor drunkards nor slanderers nor swindlers will inherit the kingdom of God. And that is what some of you were. But you were washed, you were sanctified, you were justified in the name of the Lord Jesus Christ and by the Spirit of our God" (1 Cor. 6:9–11). The key phrase is "And that is what some of you were". But something drastic and radical has happened. The finished work has happened! You were washed from all your sins and made clean. You were set apart for God and made perfect, holy and complete in Christ (Heb. 10:14). You have been made righteous because God made him who had no sin to be sin for us, so that in him we might become the righteousness of God (2 Cor. 5:21). (6) If truth sets free, what keeps us in bondage? LIES! That's why I wanted you to work through the Freedom From Addiction Workbook as it will not only show you the truth that sets free, but the lies you are believing that keep you in bondage. (7) Of course your wife wants you to be a loving husband who is patient and kind. All wives want that. My wife has let me know that many times, BUT if you focus on patience and kindness you are absolutely off track. Patience and kindness are fruits of the Holy Spirit (Gal. 5:22, 23), they will not be found in you but in Christ who is your life (Col. 3:4) and are not available anywhere else. But the good news is that Patience and Kindness lives in you. Christ is living in you and is your life, and until you understand, know and believe that it will not make any difference what you do. You might learn a few coping skills and hold it together temporarily, but it won't last. (8) As I said in my last email to you, I found my freedom from alcoholism 32 years ago when I believed Gal. 2:20. In the past few years I have learned a lot more about who I am in Christ and more important who Christ is in me. That is the issue. "To whom God was pleased to give knowledge of the wealth of the glory of this secret among the Gentiles, which is Christ in you, the hope of glory:" (Col. 1:27 BBE). If Christ is in me and is living in me as Gal. 2:20 so clearly says, "I have been put to death on the cross with Christ; still I am living; no longer I, but Christ is living in me; and that life which I now am living in the flesh I am living by faith, the faith of the Son of God, who in love for me, gave himself up for me." (Gal. 2:20 BBE), that is a game changer. That is the earth shaking, liberating truth that sets free. If Christ is in me, what else could I possibly need? We have it ALL! We have EVERYTHING!!! We very seldom feel like it, look like it or act like it, but that doesn't alter the TRUTH in any way. We absolutely have to get our focus off ourselves and our behavior and our feelings and look to the TRUTH, who is Jesus. I believe that you have decided on your course of action and that's fine. As I have laid out here, I do not agree with it but I don't need to. You said that you hadn't read the articles because so much was going on and you didn't have time, but you found time to watch the movie twice. I'm not criticizing you as I firmly believe you need to follow through on what you believe will work for you and that is what you are doing. If you don't, you will just be going through the motions and we have all done that too many times. You have to do what you believe you should do. God will work all of it out for good. I will be praying for you and am available to you if you want to talk. But please don't think you need to check in with me. Just follow through with what you're doing.

P. S. If you disagree with me, don't think you have to let me know. There are quite a few people who don't agree with me. I don't have much interest in theological dialogues. I'm probably too old anyway. I am 83, have been a Christian for 50 years, a former pastor, seminary graduate, but NOT an alcoholic and have been in the school of hard knocks for a long time, but haven't graduated yet and God is working all things together for my good and also yours (Rom. 8:28).

Note: Unfortunately, and very sadly, this man who had become a friend of mine had a heart attack and died a few weeks later. There is no doubt that he was very sincere and wanted to be whom he believed God wanted him to be, a loving, faithful, patient and kind husband that his wife so desired. The problem was not that he wasn't sincere and committed, but simply that he did not believe the truth that sets free (John 8:32).

Do you not believe that drinking alcohol is a sin? Many teach that it is?

No, I do not believe that drinking alcohol is a sin and I believe the Scripture is very clear on that. If drinking alcohol is a sin, then Jesus committed a sin and we know that he did not. "The Son of Man came eating and drinking, and they say, 'Look at him! A glutton and a drunkard, a friend of tax collectors and sinners!' Yet wisdom is justified by her deeds" (Matt. 11:19 ESV). The Apostle Paul confirmed this when he said, "No longer drink only water, but use a little wine for the sake of your stomach and your frequent ailments" (1 Tim. 5:23 ESV). However, getting drunk is a sin as Eph. 5:18 says, "And do not get drunk with wine, for that is debauchery, but be filled with the Spirit" (Eph. 5:18 ESV). I usually keep wine and beer in the refrigerator and have some now and then, but often go a month or so without it.

How can we be filled with the Spirit and not get drunk?

Good question! Anything that we get from God is always and only by faith. Martin Luther said, "If you believe you shall have all things. If you do not believe, you shall lack all things. That which is impossible for you to accomplish by trying to fulfill all the works of the law—many and useless as they all are—you will accomplish quickly and easily through faith. God our Father has made all things depend on faith so that whoever has faith has all things and whoever does not have faith will have nothing…. Thus the promises of God give what the law prescribes so that all things may be God's alone, both the commandments and the fulfilling of the commandments. He alone commands, He alone fulfills." The commandment is to be filled with the Holy Spirit. The promise is that "Whoever believes in me, as the Scripture has said, streams of living water will flow from within him. By this he meant the Spirit, whom those who believed in him were later to receive. Up to that time the Spirit had not been given, since Jesus had not yet been glorified" (John 7:38, 39). Yes, we have received the Holy Spirit who lives in us and our only response is to believe. That is all we are called on (commanded?) to do. When the disciples came to Jesus and said, "What shall we do, so that we may work the works of God?" Jesus answered and said to them, "This is the work of God, that you believe in Him whom He has sent." (John 6:38, 39 NASB). I will freely admit that it is not easy to believe that we no longer live but Jesus Christ, the Son of God lives in us and we now live by faith, but when we believe that simple statement is when we are filled with the Holy Spirit and experience the peace, freedom, joy and fulfillment that has been given to us. There is nothing to intend, nothing to attempt, nothing to obtain but simply to believe the truth that you are accepted, forgiven, loved, blessed, righteous, holy and freed from any and all bondage.

It has been awhile since I reached out to you about my marriage and our separation. It appears my husband sees no future for us except "hopelessness". A friend of mine asked me to research "narcissism" and WOW... most of the characteristics are classic. Have you dealt with this and is it likely he can or will change? I realize that is a blanket question and probably a bit unfair, but have you had any dealings with this?

You asked "is it likely he can or will change?" The answer is No and Yes. As for narcissism, everyone in the world is narcissistic apart from Christ. It is defined as excessive interest in oneself and extreme selfishness. Everyone on the face of this earth, apart from Christ, is self-centered. Some are better at hiding it than others, and some are so wrapped up in themselves that most can't stand to be around them. Of course, many Christians do not know who they are in Christ and what they have in Him and are narcissistic. In other words, they are living in deception and at times are very narcissistic. The essence of addiction is self-consciousness and everyone with an addictive behavior is completely self-centered, which is a major part of the problem. So, the answer is "no" if your husband is not in Christ. The answer is "yes" if he is in Christ and knows Christ is in him and is his life. In other words, if he knows and believes Gal. 2:20 "I have been put to death on the cross with Christ; still I am living; no longer I, but Christ is living in me; and that life which I now am living in the flesh I am living by faith, the faith of the Son of God, who in love for me, gave himself up for me."(Gal. 2:20 BBE). That is the only way anyone can or will change. In fact, all Christians have been changed and are new creations who are dead to sin and freed from it. But as I said, most Christians are living in deception as I was for the first 18 years of my Christian life.

37

What does it mean to "believe"?

Webster's defines "believe" as to exercise belief in; to credit upon the authority or testimony of another; to be persuaded of the truth of, to have a firm persuasion, esp. of the truths of religion. Biblical belief means that you believe God, and when we do believe His word it changes everything… our life and how we live and our relationships and what we do and do not do. "And we also thank God continually because, when you received the word of God, which you heard from us, you accepted it not as the word of men, but as it actually is, the word of God, which is at work in you who believe" (1 Thess. 2:13). I found my freedom from alcoholism 32 years ago when I believed Gal. 2:20. In these last years I have learned a lot more about who I am in Christ and more important who Christ is in me. That is the issue. "To them God has chosen to make known among the Gentiles the glorious riches of this mystery, which is Christ in you, the hope of glory" (Col. 1:27). The glorious riches of the mystery have been made known. It is Christ in me and He is living in me as Gal. 2:20 so clearly says. That is a game changer. That is the earthshaking, liberating truth that sets free. I have never seen anyone get free who did not believe Gal. 2:20. There is nothing to do. It has been done! IT IS FINISHED!!! As Jesus told Jairus the Synagogue ruler when they told him his daughter was dead, "don't be afraid; just believe" (Mark 5:36). If Christ is living in me, what else could I possibly need? I have it ALL! I have EVERYTHING!!! We very seldom feel like it, look like it or act like it, but that doesn't alter the TRUTH in any way. We absolutely have to get our focus off ourselves and our behavior and our feelings and look to the TRUTH, who is Jesus who said, "then you will know the truth, and the truth will set you free" (John 8:32 NIV). As Martin Luther said, "The law says 'do this and never is it done'. Grace says, 'Believe in this One and it is already done.'" AMEN!

38

Up to this point, not one of the few people to whom I have proclaimed this truth has been set free. I am feeling that this truth must be revealed to each individual by the Holy Spirit. We have prayed and proclaimed, but is it not true this requires the individual to cast themselves upon Christ in such a manner that they are desperately dependent on His working and solely trusting that He alone can deliver them???

I feel your pain. Seriously, I do understand as I have experienced what you describe many times in the last 32 years I have been in this ministry. It is a "niche" ministry and we will never see the numbers and results that we would like to see. You write, "I am feeling that this truth must be revealed to each individual by the Holy Spirit. We have prayed and proclaimed, but is it not true this requires the individual to cast themselves upon Christ in such a manner that they are desperately dependent on His working and solely trusting that He alone can deliver them?" The answer is yes. You also said that they must be"desperately dependent". That is the key. The truth must be revealed by the Holy Spirit, but "Desperation is the key to revelation." In other words, they must get to a place where they absolutely come to the end of self and know beyond a shadow of doubt that there is nothing they can do to get free, live the Christian life, etc. That is brokenness. Even though most of their lives seem to be shattered beyond belief, they still harbor some belief that there is something they can do to get free, which of course is a lie. I have found over the years that there is nothing I can do or say that will help them. As long as they have a shred of belief that there is something they can do to help themselves, they must give it a shot and find out for themselves that there is nothing that they can do. I'm working with a man right now who is a very wealthy and accomplished individual. His wife that he loves very much has left him; I keep telling him the "truth that sets free" and it is as if I'm talking to a wall. I talked to him last night and I've learned over the years that all I can do is love and accept him, pray for him and be available, but let him do what he has to do to learn that there is nothing he can do. I don't agree with AA on most things, but one saying they have that I agree with is, "It takes what it takes". Yes, it does and what it takes is brokenness. 2 Cor. 1:8, 9 puts it like this "We do not want you to be uninformed, brothers, about the hardships we suffered in the province of Asia. We were under great pressure, far beyond our ability to endure, so that we despaired even of life. Indeed, in our hearts we felt the sentence of death. But this happened that we might not rely on ourselves but on God, who raises the dead" (2 Cor. 1:8–9 NIV). I keep saying that the answer to addiction (really the answer to everything) is to know Christ is your life and that you are dead to sin and freed from it, BUT no one will be able to believe and trust Christ as their life until they give up on their life. As it says, "that we might not rely on ourselves but on God, who raises the dead". This ministry has many ups and downs and more downs than ups, but when I see someone believe "the truth that sets free" and experience "so if the Son sets you free, you will be free indeed" (John 8:32), it makes it all more than worthwhile. I would not have chosen this ministry, but God has called me to it and there is nothing else that I can do and I find such fulfillment as I do so.

I've struggled with an addiction for a looooonnnnng time and while I have had days of freedom, I have never had a consistent total victory. I have tried everything and even did your on-line webinar, but still...no joy. Joseph Prince, in his book "The Power of Right Believing", basically teaches that "we are the righteousness of God in Christ Jesus" and that if we keep confessing that we will eventually get freedom. I have run out of options and every time I hear something "new" that I haven't tried I think to myself that this is it, I will finally get free, only to be disappointed. Is there still any hope for me?

It is actually very good that you have run out of "options" as your options are things that you have tried, and as long as you think there is something you can do and are trying, you will not receive God's answer (which has been provided for you and is already yours to believe and receive). I am very familiar with Joseph Prince and "we are the righteousness of God in Christ Jesus" and it is good to confess that, but as Rom. 10:6-10 says "But the righteousness that is by faith says, "Do not say in your heart, 'Who will ascend into heaven?'" (that is, to bring Christ down) "or 'Who will descend into the deep?'" (that is, to bring Christ up from the dead). But what does it say? "The word is near you; it is in your mouth and in your heart," that is, the word of faith we are proclaiming: That if you confess with your mouth, "Jesus is Lord," and believe in your heart that God raised him from the dead, you will be saved. For it is with your heart that you believe and are justified, and it is with your mouth that you confess and are saved." The key here is that you BELIEVE with your heart, then you confess with your mouth. You don't do anything to be the righteousness of God in Jesus Christ as you already are. Here again the key is the title of the book, The Power of Right Believing. Of course, the problem is that we are trying to get to the point where we feel we are dead to sin and freed from it (Rom. 6:6, 7) which will never happen. I don't feel like I am dead to sin and freed from it, but it is still true and I can choose by faith to believe it. As Jesus told Jairus, the Synagogue ruler, when they told him his daughter was dead, Don't be afraid, just believe (Mark 5:36).

What about the physical aspect of addiction? I believe that my smoking is an addiction. Doesn't the physical aspect of addiction have to be addressed?

You are most likely correct in that your smoking is an addiction. In most cases addiction has three aspects; physical, emotional and spiritual. There is nothing wrong in using what God has provided to deal with the physical aspect, such as doctors and medicine, but in most addiction the physical aspect is an extremely small part of the addiction. For instance, in drug and alcohol addiction secular treatment centers can detox people in a week and take care of the physical aspect, but that has barely begun to address the issue. People are primarily addicted to substances because of the emotional and spiritual aspects. The emotional aspect includes the fact that it has become habitual, but more importantly it is enjoyable and a way to deal with stress. But the spiritual aspect is by far the biggest aspect of the addiction and must be dealt with if a person is to experience freedom, which only God provides. At its core, addiction is spiritual bondage. By that I mean that a person is believing Satan's lies about his identity. I believed that I was insecure, inadequate, inferior and guilty, but when I believed that Christ was my life and was living it, I experienced my freedom. Of course, some are able to cope and get sober and clean but do not experience freedom.

Freedom is only experienced when a person understands and believes who they are in Christ and that they no longer live but Christ lives in them and they now live by faith (Gal 2:20). Freedom has been provided for every born-again believer through the finished work of Christ, but it seems few of them are experiencing it. When a person believes the truth of who they are in Christ and they are dead to sin and freed from it (Rom. 6:6, 7), Christ is their life (Col. 3:4) and they are one spirit with Him (1 Cor. 6:17), they are really free John 8:32, 36). Unfortunately, no secular program and few Christian recovery ministries address this issue and that is why addiction is so rampant and why few are finding freedom from addiction. Addiction is primarily spiritual bondage and few recovery ministries understand that and address it. A person must know and believe who they are in Christ to experience freedom from addiction. It is simply an issue of believing "the truth that sets free" and as long as a person is doing what he thinks he should do, they will never experience their freedom. They might learn some ways of coping and be clean and sober for a while, but freedom is available only through the finished work of Christ.

What about casting out a demon? Don't you believe that the demonic is involved in addiction and that a "power encounter" is needed?

I am not saying that a "power encounter" will not work. What I am saying is that unless a person knows the truth of who they are in Christ and what they have in Christ, there is nothing to prevent the demon from coming back. The "truth encounter" is the Biblical way of deliverance. The truth that a Christian is seated with Christ in the heavenly places, is dead to sin, freed from sin, that Christ is their life and they are one spirit with Him is the "truth that sets free" and what every Christian needs to know. Sadly, most of them don't know it and are not free in Christ. One-third of Jesus' ministry was deliverance, BUT that was before the cross and His finished work. Now every Christian is crucified, dead, buried and raised up as a new creation and they no longer live, but Christ is living in them. The only real weapon Satan has against the believer is deception. Scripture says "the devil is not holding to the truth, for there is no truth in him. When he lies, he speaks his native language, for he is a liar and the father of lies" (John 8:44). Yes, he is the Liar of all liars and is very good at it and keeps many from experiencing their freedom in Christ. When we know the truth of "Christ in you" we experience freedom. I have worked with quite a few people who were "demonized", and those who believed the truth of who they were in Christ and that they were dead to sin and the law found their freedom. BUT not until then, and only then.

What about prescription meds? I am on antidepressants and thinking about getting off them by going cold turkey. What would be your advice on this?

I really cannot in good conscience give you any advice on prescription medications. A medical doctor prescribes them and I do not know what your physical condition is or your emotional or spiritual condition for that matter. I am 83 years old and take a few prescription drugs myself. Whereas I believe as you do that healing is provided for us through the finished work of Christ (Isa. 53:4, 5), but all of our bodies are different and all of us have different needs and issues. For instance, I believe some are more prone to depression and I have seen them profit from anti-depressants. I also believe that some of us have a genetic predisposition to more likely become addicted to alcohol and/or drugs. However, that genetic predisposition is in our body and we are spiritual entities. We must remember that we are not physical beings who have received a spirit, but are spiritual beings who live in a body. In other words, your body is not who you are. One of these days our physical body will wear out and go to the dust, but that is not the end of us. As Jesus told Martha, "I am the resurrection and the life. He who believes in me will live, even though he dies; and whoever lives and believes in me will never die. Do you believe this?" I realize I haven't answered your question, but I really cannot give you medical advice. I would not recommend going cold turkey but rather get some solid medical advice.

43

I am addicted to pain medication (Oxycontin). These are prescribed and without them I am in severe pain. But here is my dilemma, I do not know if the Lord wants me to give these pain meds up or not? The obvious answer is: "Ask God." But, I have and I am just not sure I am hearing from Him or not. Since asking Him, I have been reading a lot about 'idols' and also repentance. Then I try to go off them and the excruciating pain sets in and I return to taking them and at the same time, as a result of my long term illness, my life has fallen apart. I have other health issues that are so debilitating that without pain meds I would be bedridden. But I keep on having to up my dose or they don't work. Seems like they are a horrible lie from Satan. I have been like this for five years and most of my relationships have not survived and my home is under threat of the bank.

I am not sure I can answer your question, but I do want to address some issues you brought up.

(1) First you mentioned idols. Forget that. You need to concentrate on "the truth that sets free". You have been

forgiven and there is no condemnation. You are in Christ and He is in you. There is only one thing that keeps Christians in bondage and that is deception, because as scripture clearly tells us It was for freedom that Christ set us free (Gal. 5 :1) and "For we know that our old self was crucified with him so that the body of sin might be done away with, that we should no longer be slaves to sin — because anyone who has died has been freed from sin." (Rom. 6:6–7 NIV). There is no more condemnation, guilt, judgment, or punishment (Rom. 8:2).

(2) The above is a simple basic truth, but when a person really believes, it is when they experience their freedom that has been provided for them. Repentance is not doing anything. It is simply turning from lies to believe the truth and the truth is that you are dead to the law (that's grace) and you are dead to sin and freed from it (that's who you are in Christ).

(3) As for guilt, there is no such thing for a Christian unless the cross of Christ didn't work. IT IS FINISHED!!! Are Christians guilty? NOT unless the cross didn't work and Jesus didn't accomplish what He came to do. The last judgment for the Christian was at the cross. The truth is that there is no more sin, death, condemnation or guilt, "Therefore, there is now no condemnation for those who are in Christ Jesus, because through Christ Jesus the law of the Spirit of life set me free from the law of sin and death" (Rom. 8:1,2). All the guilt, shame, and condemnation you feel is just deception. It is not even real. It is a lie from Satan. As for whether you should quit cold turkey, probably not. If you do try to quit, you should do it under a doctor's orders and supervision. God is in everything, including doctors, drugs, diseases, etc. And also, you need to realize that all our bodies are different, but your body is NOT who you are. You are a spiritual being who lives in a body. I am 83 and have insomnia, which plagues many of us old people. I

have to take a sleeping pill to sleep. God does love you and there is nothing you can do to make Him love you more or anything you can do that will make Him love you less. It is a done deal. You are forgiven, loved, accepted, righteous, holy and blameless no matter what you do, how you feel or how you look or what anybody says. "DON'T BE AFRAID, JUST BELIEVE!" (Mark 5:36). One final thought is that you have an illness and are bedridden, so you should follow your doctor's orders about what to take and not to take.

You quote John 8:32 a lot "Then you will know the truth, and the truth will set you free." But what about John 8:31 that says if you continue in the word then you will know the truth. Don't those two verses go together?

Of course, verses 31 and 32 go together. What does it mean to continue in His word? It primarily means that you believe in Jesus Christ as your Lord and Savior, which of course every Christian has done. If you have received Christ as your Lord and Savior, then you have "Christ in you who is your life" (Col. 3:4); "you are one spirit with Him" (1 Cor. 6:17); "you are dead to sin and freed from it" (Rom. 6:6, 7); "you have been crucified with Christ and you no longer live, but Christ is living in you" (Gal. 2:20) and cannot get any freer. They will experience more freedom when they know and believe the truth. By the way, I really am not interested in theological wrangling and arguments. I have been a Christian for 50 years and I am only interested in helping Christians find their freedom in Christ, and when they know and believe those verses above and that Christ is living their life is when they discover it. May the Lord bless you and all who read this and may you experience all the peace, joy and freedom that is yours in Christ. The absolutely amazing and incredible thing is that it has all been done and all we have to do is believe the truth. "Your life is hidden with Christ in God" (Col. 3:3). And always remember it is not talking about words written on a page in the Bible. To continue in His Word is to believe the truth, and the truth is that you are free. Also remember that Jesus is the Word, "in the beginning was the Word, and the Word was with God, and the Word was God" (John 1:1). The truth is that every Christian is completely free and will never get any freer, but will be able to experience it when they believe the truth that sets free.

It seems to me that the reason for people struggling with addictive behavior is that they have not grown and matured in the Christian life and do not understand and know what will bring joy in their life.

I don't think you understand our approach. First of all, if your belief that addiction is a maturity issue then what are you going to do to get the person to mature. You will have to get them to "do" things to get there. You will have to put them under law to get to that point. That approach is really no different from all the 12-step programs. The focus is on the person and what they do with the implication that the person needs to shape up and get his act together and do right. It bypasses the truth that the old person is dead, buried and gone and that there is nothing we can do to shape him up. "Therefore if anyone is in Christ, he is a new creature; the old things passed away; behold, new things have come" (2 Cor. 5:17). Your approach assumes that they are addicted because they don't know what will bring joy, but it is actually because they don't know the truth of who they are in Christ. They don't understand what the finished work of Christ has provided for them. You say the New Testament is entirely focused on one thing - how you are going to mature. I believe the New Testament is focused on one thing - God in man (Christ in you), that is the New Covenant and when a person understands that Christ is his life and lives in him and he is a new creation, who is dead to sin and freed from it, he will be free indeed (John 8:36). Satan's plan is to keep you from believing the truth that sets you free (John 8:32). He is the father of lies and deception is really his only weapon against the believer.

It seems you don't recognize the demonic factor in addiction and downplay spiritual warfare. Don't you think the demonic should be addressed?

You say I downplay spiritual warfare and you are right to some degree. I was on staff with Dr. Neil Anderson and Freedom in Christ Ministries for 12 years and we knew that spiritual warfare was a "truth encounter", not a power encounter; we didn't address the demonic but taught the person the truth. In literally many thousands of sessions we found that was the only thing that worked. Neil lays it out in his book, "The Bondage Breaker". I'm not sure what you mean by I teach that if you absorb the truth, you will be free. What I teach is that if you believe the truth, you will be free as Jesus said, "Then you will know the truth, and the truth will make you free" (John 8:32). When you wake up in the morning and it is light outside, you know that the sun is shining, even if you can't see it for the clouds. It is the same way with the truth as feelings and circumstances do not validate the truth. You just believe the truth in your heart (See Rom. 10:8-10). The truth is that every Christian has been set free and the more he struggles to get free, mature, do right and stop sinning, the bigger hole he digs for himself. "It was for freedom that Christ set us free; therefore, keep standing firm and do not be subject again to a yoke of slavery" (Gal. 5:1). What do we need to know to be free? "For we know that our old self was crucified with him so that the body of sin might be done away with, that we should no longer be slaves to sin — because anyone who has died has been freed from sin" (Rom. 6:6, 7). The bottom line is that after being a Christian for 50 years, struggling with addiction for eight years and being free from it for 32 years, I am totally convinced that when we understand and believe Gal. 2:20 we will be really free. "I have been crucified with Christ. It is no longer I who live, but Christ who lives in me. And the life I now live in the flesh I live by faith in the Son of God, who loved me and gave himself for me" (Gal. 2:20). If a person knows and believes: (1) the old self is crucified, dead and gone and he no longer lives, but Christ lives in him and is his life and he lives by faith in that truth and (2) that he is dead to sin and freed from it, then what else does he need but to believe the truth? I could go on, but obviously we understand this very differently. One final thing I would say is that until a person comes to the end of self and their resources and experiences brokenness, he is unable to believe the truth of who he is and what he has in Christ. You absolutely must come to the end of self-effort and your wisdom and strength. You cannot trust Christ's life in you until you give up on your life.

I have read in a devotional by a famous author to pray, read the bible, memorize scripture, go to church, and resist temptation and I will eventually get free from my addiction. Are you saying that this will not help?

I don't really want to be negative and critical, but this is the kind of counsel that most Christians struggling with addictive behavior receive and it does not even begin to help them. It is pure "reformed theology", which basically says "stop sinning and do right". This is the teaching on counseling that I received in seminary. The problem is that the person cannot do that because they are in spiritual bondage and the only way they will do it is to believe the truth of who they are in Christ and that they are dead to sin and freed from it. I have a webinar I call, "The Strongholds of Addiction - The Lies that Keep us in bondage" (See next question and answer). Those four strongholds are:

(1) The Stronghold of Hopelessness and Low Self-Esteem

(2) The Stronghold of Shame and Guilt

(3) The Stronghold of Insecurity and Rejection

(4) The Stronghold of Self-help (Legalism)

They have absolutely nothing to do with the addictive behavior itself, which is just a manifestation of the stronghold. The author you referred to begins with a verse in the Old Testament that says we will walk in freedom because of what we do, "I have sought your precepts". He quotes John 8:32, "you will know the truth and the truth will set you free" and correctly says that it is about freedom from the slavery of sin, but doesn't tell us what that truth is. He quotes 2 Pet. 1:4 which I quote a lot "Through these he has given us his very great and precious promises, so that through them you may participate in the divine nature and escape the corruption in the world caused by evil desires." I believe it is a prescription for freedom from addiction. But He doesn't point out what sets us free, that we are "partakers of the divine nature". As a result of the finished work of Christ, that is who we are - "I have been crucified with Christ and I no longer live, but Christ lives in me. The life I live in the body, I live by faith in the Son of God, who loved me and gave himself for me." (Gal. 2:20 NIV). As Rom. 6:6, 7 says "For we know that our old self was crucified with him so that the body of sin might be done away with, that we should no longer be slaves to sin — because anyone who has died has been freed from sin" (Rom. 6:6–7 NIV). When a person believes who they are in Christ and what they have in Christ, they walk free. Pure "reformed theology" has three major flaws and I had to change my theology to get free. The three major flaws I see are: (1) Reformed theology is also called "covenant theology". They do not make a clear distinction between the Old Covenant and the New Covenant. They don't really see the New Covenant as totally new, but as a new and improved Old Covenant. Therefore, they do not make a clear distinction between law and grace, which I believe is absolutely essential to experience freedom in Christ. You must know and believe that you are dead to the law (Rom. 7:4) and redeemed from it (Gal. 3:15) and are no longer under it (Rom. 6:14) to be free. We must understand grace to experience our freedom. Only when you know and believe that God has done it all for you will you experience your freedom. (2) They believe that sanctification is achieved by "obeying the law", not by faith. Of course, you have the Holy Spirit to help you, but it is up to you. That is "works sanctification" whereas sanctification is achieved by faith through grace (Acts 26:18, 2 Thess. 2:13). (3) They believe that the identity of a Christian is "a sinner saved by grace" and some even refer to them as a worm. If we believe we are a sinner, then what do we do, we sin. If we believe we are an alcoholic (addict), what do we do, we drink and drug and get drunk or high or white knuckle it trying not to. Neither is a very satisfactory way to live. When we believe who we are in Christ and that Christ is our life and we are dead to sin and freed from it is when we live free from addiction and all bondage.

What are the four strongholds of addiction and where do you find that in scripture?

There is an undisputed problem of addiction in this nation and worldwide. More money has been thrown at the problem, but the addiction problem seems to be exponentially increasing. There are basically two reasons for this. First is that it is a spiritual problem and demands a spiritual answer and very few are offering that. Addiction is basically spiritual bondage, and the only answer is found through the finished work of Christ through a personal relationship with Christ that begins when we receive Him as Lord and Savior. When we realize that Christ is our life and begin to lay hold of who we are in Christ (our true identity as a born-again believer), we begin to walk free. It sounds simple, and it actually is, but few Christians ever lay hold of this. That is why so many struggle with addiction, including myself. I struggled with addiction to alcohol for eight long miserable years in a nightmare I couldn't wake up from (see my testimony in the Appendix, "The Strange Odyssey of a Legalistic Preacher Who Became a Drunk, Discovered Grace and Was Set Free"). The second reason is that by and large people have no understanding of the real issue. Why do I say that? Because most of the treatment centers (secular and Christian), counselors, pastors, recovery ministries method of dealing with the issue is behavior modification, but if the issue is spiritual bondage, which it is, then no behavior change will touch the problem. I know as I tried at least 30 different changes of behavior, which didn't help, but only exacerbated the issue. If we will take a look at the 4 Hebrew words in Proverbs 31:6-7: (Perishing, Anguish, Poverty and Misery) we will understand what the problem of addiction is and why so few are finding their freedom. "It is not for kings, O Lemuel — not for kings to drink wine, not for rulers to crave beer, lest they drink and forget what the law decrees, and deprive all the oppressed of their rights. 6 Give beer to those who are perishing, wine to those who are in anguish; 7 let them drink and forget their poverty and remember their misery no more." (Prov. 31:4-7). Here are the four Strongholds of Addiction that are the root causes of addiction that most programs never address and why so few people are finding freedom.

1. Perishing – to lose oneself, fail, be undone, be destroyed, to be forgotten, have no way to flee:

The Stronghold of Hopelessness and Low Self-Esteem.

The Lie—I am the same old, sin-loving sinner who is helpless and hopeless and will never change. I cannot do what I should do and keep doing the things I should not do. I am unable to do what I should and get free from addiction. As long as a person believes this lie it will make no difference what they do. I know as I prayed, studied, fasted, memorized chapters of scripture and my addiction seemed to spiral out of control no matter what I did. I memorized Romans 6 and Colossians 3 which I believe are the two best chapters in the bible on freedom all to no avail. But when I believed a half of a verse in Rom. 6:1 that I had died to sin, I was freed from my addiction. Malcolm Smith ("Spiritual Strongholds") testifies that he memorized the whole New Testament and didn't find his freedom. The problem is that we always act consistently and persistently with whom we perceive ourselves to be. Who do you perceive yourself to be?

The Truth—The old person I used to be was crucified with Christ (Rom 6:4). I am a new creation (2 Cor 5:17), who is dead to sin (Rom 6:2) and freed from it (Rom. 6:6, 7). I am a righteous saint (2 Cor. 5:21). When a person believes this truth is when he walks free. Am I saying that I live a perfect life and don't sin. No, but I am saying that I believed this truth 32 years ago and have been free from addiction ever since.

2. Anguish - bitter, provoked, grieved, vexed & discontented:

The Stronghold of Shame

The Lie—I keep doing wrong and I deserve to be condemned and punished and I can't face the truth about myself. I am a prisoner of my past. More than likely Satan's biggest lie is that we are still sin-loving sinners and we should be judged, punished and condemned. Basically, Satan is telling us that the cross did not work and we are guilty and condemned. Why can't we believe that IT IS FINISHED?! As long as a person believes this lie they will live in bondage. When we understand and believe what the finished work of Christ accomplished and that our old sinner self was crucified, dead, buried and gone (Gal. 2:20) is when we will begin to live free. How? Because we are free, "It is for freedom that Christ has set us free…" (Gal. 5:1).

The Truth—There is no more guilt and condemnation in Christ (Rom. 8:1). Sin has been taken care of and is no more. IT IS FINISHED! God has taken care of my past in the cross and I am now a product of the cross.

3. Poverty – to be destitute, have lack, needy, poor:

The Stronghold of Insecurity and Rejection

The Lie—I am unloved and unaccepted because I have sinned and messed up so much and have been forsaken and am without support. I am at the mercy of Satan, who jerks me around and makes my life miserable.

The Truth—God loves me deeply and totally accepts me and will never leave me or forsake me (Heb. 13:5,6) and has given me everything I need for life and godliness (2 Pet 1:3), every spiritual blessing (Eph 1:3), freedom (Rom. 6:6, 7) and victory (1 Cor 15:57). I am a child of God and greater is He who is in you than he who is in the world (1 John 4:4 NASB) and the evil one cannot harm me (1 John 5:18).

4. Misery – to toil severely with irksome, wearying effort:

The Stronghold of Legalism (Self-help) See Galatians 3:1-5

The Lie—It is up to me and I cannot do it. I have tried and tried and failed and I am giving out. I can't live the Christian life, do what I am supposed to do and get free from addiction.

The Truth—God will do it all for me (1 Thess. 5:24) and has called me to give up (2 Cor 1:8,9) and rest in Him (Heb. 4:10). Christ has set me free (Gal. 5:1) and I am dead to sin (Rom. 6:2) and freed from it (Rom. 6:7) Christ is in me and I am in Him (John 14:20) and I can trust Him because He is my life (Col. 3:4).

I believe my husband is an alcoholic. He doesn't drink every day but is a binge drinker. When he is not drinking everything is OK and we get along well. What would you recommend that I do?

Just focus on Christ in you and the truth that sets free. Just let go of it all (including your marriage, etc.) and give it to Jesus who loves you completely and accepts you totally. If your behavior doesn't measure up with what you think it ought to (and it never will), just forgive yourself (and your husband) and go back to trusting God's love for you and your husband and let Him work it out for you. About the only thing we can do is trust God and believe that what He says, "And we know that in all things God works for the good of those who love him, who have been called according to his purpose." (Rom. 8:28). Here is a verse to live by and trust in when things are not going our way, "And so we know and rely on the love God has for us. God is love. Whoever lives in love lives in God, and God in him." (1 John 4:16). We can't make things work out the way we think they should. That is NOT in our job description. When the disciples came to Jesus and asked him, "'What must we do to do the works God requires?' Jesus answered, 'The work of God is this: to believe in the one he has sent.'" (John 6:28–29). As Watchman Nee once said, "The sin is always to do something". I can't tell you what to do, but as you rest in the Lord and trust Him as your life, He will lead and guide you. "For anyone who enters God's rest also rests from his own work, just as God did from his" (Heb. 4:10). I was married to my first wife for 10 years and when she asked for a divorce, I gave it to her. Did I do right? I don't know. I've been married for 45 years now and as you have read our story there have been many ups and downs, but there is no doubt that God is working all things for our good. God is love and you can rely on His love for you and trust Him with it all as you let go of it. By the way, I have a lot going on in my life and this was the message I needed to hear. I was also preaching to myself. This is the truth we can rely on (God's love for us). There really is not much else we can rely on. As Madame Guyon wrote many years ago, "Jesus is Everything. Everything else is a lie."

Does the church have an answer for addiction?

It seems that most evangelical messages these days is about Jesus being with us, for us, never leaving or forsaking us. Much is said about what He has done and will do for us. But something seems to be missing. It seems in the vast majority of these messages there is a separation between Jesus and the Christian. Most of these messages are very encouraging and uplifting but something seems to be missing. What seems to be missing reads in the Message "Trust GOD from the bottom of your heart; don't try to figure out everything on your own." (Prov. 3:5 MSG). If you figure it out on your own, you might come up with a well-reasoned theology and/or a practical program, but it will not do you much good. After three years of studying theology, Greek and Hebrew at seminary and eighteen years as a Christian I was an alcoholic and a falling down drunk. I had to change my theology to experience my freedom in Christ. Or a better way to put it I had to believe Gal. 2:20. When I believed that I was "dead to sin and freed from it" I was free. I didn't do a thing to get free. In fact, I had a hangover the day I believed the truth that I was no longer living, but Christ was living in me and I have never got over it. How could you get over it? It staggers the imagination. It blows your mind? You don't grasp it with your mind. As Rom. 10:6 says "If you confess with your mouth that Jesus is Lord and believe in your heart that God raised him from the dead, you will be saved." (Rom. 10:9 ESV). We do not believe with our minds, but our hearts. That is who you are at the core of your being (in your heart). Heart is spirit. Stop trying to figure it out and as Jesus responded to Jairus when they told him his daughter was dead, "Ignoring what they said, Jesus told the synagogue ruler, "Don't be afraid; just believe."(Mark 5:36 NIV). Ignore the facts, the circumstances, your feelings, what others say and believe Jesus (The TRUTH).

Do you think I'm wrong in saying that a person struggling with an addiction is not born again and a believer in Christ?

Yes, I think you are wrong on this. I do not think the problem is that they are not born again. Neil Anderson has said that 90% of Christian are not experiencing their freedom because they are believing a lie. I am a prime example as I had been a Christian for 18 years and was a seminary graduate and a former pastor who was struggling with addiction. I have talked to hundreds of Christians who are struggling with addictions in the 32 years I have been free from my addiction. I don't think they would have been talking to me if they were not born again. I don't think you would ask the question if you were not born again. We need to realize that Satan is the ruler of this world (1 John 5:19) and is the father of lies and that is really his only weapon against the Christian, but it is the only one he needs to keep us in bondage. We need to realize that any Christian who is in bondage is deceived. How could we be in bondage if Christ is in the Father and we are in Christ and Christ is in us and living in us? Bondage = Deception! There are many Christians struggling with the bondage of addiction who do not know or believe who they are in Christ and that they have been set free from all bondage.

What about going to a treatment center??

I have a list of over 100 Christian treatment centers and refer people to them from time to time. I always do it with a disclaimer, that no program or treatment center can set you free. I do not have a program that can set you free. Oswald Chambers once said, "The only valid ministry is to point people to Christ". My ministry is to point people to Christ, "so if the Son makes you free, you will be free indeed" (John 8:36) and I point people (Christians) to "Christ in them" (Gal. 2:20). There are times when it is beneficial for a person to go into treatment to get away from the stress and pressures they are facing. I went to a secular treatment center and a Christian treatment center. I don't think I got much out of the secular center, except I was without alcohol for 30 days. The Christian treatment center I attended was a 60-day program; I didn't learn the "truth that sets free" but God used it in my life and my marriage. It probably saved my marriage. My wife saw that I was serious about my problem and was willing to do what I could to find a solution. I never recommend secular centers, but if that is what a person has decided to do, I don't discourage them from doing so. We need to realize that God is not limited by anything, including AA and secular treatment centers, and can work in the individual regardless. The problem with most Christian treatment centers is that they tend to be legalistic, as most churches do. They tell you what you should do and, in most cases, they are excellent things to do such as prayer, bible reading, study, and memorization. But the problem is that we are set free not by what we do, but by what we believe (the truth that sets free). I did all those things. I usually had a two-hour quiet time, lots of prayer, Bible study, discipleship groups, fasting, etc. I memorized the two best chapters in the bible on freedom in Christ (Romans 6 and Colossians 3). All to no avail. It is not what we do, read, memorize and have a knowledge of but what we believe. When I believed two verses, I was free from addiction and have been for 32 years. For we know that our old self was crucified with him so that the body of sin might be done away with, that we should no longer be slaves to sin — because anyone who has died has been freed from sin. (Rom. 6:6,7) HALLELUJAH, what a Savior!!!

You really emphasize grace to the extent that there is nothing for us to do, but believe that God has done it all. Surely there is something we need to be doing such as prayer, bible study and reading, etc. to get our freedom and maintain it, isn't it?

I think you have hit on the major reason and the lie and mis-perception that most Christians have that keep them in bondage. This book is about the astounding truth that we possess God's answer for addiction (besetting sin, life-controlling problem, thorn in the flesh). This book is about the simple fact that all of what we need and desire in the Christian life (peace, freedom, joy and victory) is by and through grace. In other words, it is by God, through Him and up to Him. In fact, it has already been done. The best definition of grace is "God has done it". It is finished! All of our struggling, striving and straining is counter productive and effectively keeps us from experiencing it. We labor under the deception that it is up to us to live the Christian life and make it work. Nothing could be further from the truth. Most of us struggle to overcome the issue that weighs us down, and it continually defeats us and robs us of our freedom. We exert all our efforts to get our act together and shape up to no avail. But the startling truth is that the problem is the solution. When we realize that we cannot get our act together and shape up and never will, we are ready for God's answer. We can't get our act together because as Romans 7:18 tells us For I know that nothing good dwells in me, that is, in my flesh; for the willing is present in me, but the doing of the good is not. We cannot get our act together because it is flesh, and it doesn't make any difference how willing we are because there is nothing good in it. It is only when we know that apart from Christ we can do nothing and embrace our weakness and look to Him can we experience the freedom that is ours in Christ. It really is always all of grace, and that means it is none of us. Paul experienced this when he said, Because of the surpassing greatness of the revelations, for this reason, to keep me from exalting myself, there was given me a thorn in the flesh, a messenger of Satan to torment me—to keep me from exalting myself! Concerning this, I implored the Lord three times that it might leave me. And He has said to me, "My grace is sufficient for you, for power is perfected in weakness." Most gladly, therefore, I will rather boast about my weaknesses, so that the power of Christ may dwell in me. Therefore, I am well content with weaknesses, with insults, with distresses, with persecutions, with difficulties, for Christ's sake; for when I am weak, then I am strong. (2 Cor. 12:7-10). Every Christian struggles with some issue or problem in his life that keeps him from experiencing peace, freedom and joy. It may be a hurtful habit, an addiction, a life-controlling problem, a besetting sin or a thorn in the flesh. When he can realize it really is all of grace and embrace his weakness and look to Christ he has found his answer. As one country pastor purportedly said, "Your problem is you don't know what your problem is. You think your problem is your problem, but that's not the problem at all. Your problem is not your problem, and that's your main problem". Until we understand that the addictive behavior of alcoholism, drug and/or sex addiction, etc. is not the problem, but the false identity we have in the flesh, we will not make any headway. No one will experience freedom in Christ until they know the old self they were was crucified with Christ and is no more (Gal. 2:20) and that Christ is their life (Col. 3:4) and they are dead to sin and freed from it (Rom. 6:6, 7). I still do all those things they tell us to do, Bible reading, study, memorization, Bible study groups but I don't do it to mature, get free, get closer to God, etc. I do it to fellowship with the one who loves me unconditionally and to remind myself of who I am and what have in Christ.

You asked at the webinar if I had ever been tempted to go back to my addiction and I said no. That is true, but I believe I need to clarify that.

Most of the time when people ask that they are asking "Did I ever want to drink again"? And that question really misses the point. What I mean by that is that drinking alcohol is not wrong or a sin. There are millions of people (Christians also) all over the world who will have a beer or a glass of wine or two (sometimes more) and they are not addicted, and it does not cause any problems. Of course, there are millions that their drinking causes major problems and has disastrous results. Most people (including Christians) really don't understand addiction. I'm not trying to be judgmental, but in the last 32 years I have seen few who really understand it. Let me explain it this way. I'll use alcohol as the example. The person struggling with an alcohol addiction does not drink for the same reason the non-alcoholic does. The person who is not addicted drinks for various reasons, such as to relax a little, socially (along with others) or just because he enjoys a drink or two. The alcoholic drinks to alter his mood. He is not comfortable in his own skin and who he perceives himself to be. He is drinking to achieve a result and it will take more than what an average person would drink. When he begins drinking he knows that he is probably going to lose control, but it is worth it to him to achieve the level that he needs to get to alter his mood. I speak from personal experience. I would say that 95% of the time I started drinking I knew I would probably lose control, but I did it anyway. Why would a sane person do this? Because I was temporarily insane. Addiction is spiritual bondage and is related to our identity. How we find our identity is how we meet our basic needs for 1) love and acceptance and 2) worth and value. And the way we find love and acceptance and worth and value is how we find life. That is why God's answer for addiction is to know who we are in Christ. Because LIFE IS only found in Christ, not to mention love as God is love. The average person doesn't like to lose control. They do not want to be out of control and the idea is repugnant to them. For me now it is doubly so because I know all the destruction and devastation I experienced when I struggled with my addiction to alcohol for eight long, nightmarish years. One reason the person with perfectionist flesh usually doesn't become an alcoholic or drug addict is that they try to control everything and the idea of losing control is abhorrent to them. So, the alcoholic is drinking alcohol for a totally different reason than the average person is. So back to me. After I found my freedom I have not been tempted to drink and lose control and I knew very well that if you drink a certain amount, you will lose control. I have not been tempted to go back to that addiction to alcohol. The issue is not have I been tempted to take a drink of alcohol as I know I am free to have a drink of alcohol if I desire one. When a person understands that the old sin-loving sinner and alcohol craving person is crucified, dead, buried and gone and who they are in Christ, what they have in Christ, that Christ is their life, that they are untied to Him and One Spirit with Him and they no longer live, but Christ lives in them it is a totally different story. Am I free to drink alcohol? Of course, I am. I am not an alcoholic and really never was. I certainly was deceived and believed that I was and acted like an alcoholic as I have documented in the books I have written. To be very truthful, I am tempted daily, but it is definitely not to abuse alcohol, get drunk and lose control. I have not lived a perfect life and my wife would confirm that, but I have been free from addiction for 32 years. By the way, my wife would also confirm that.

I have developed my own plan of intensive study, diet, exercise, vitamins, journaling and talking and listening to the Lord over the next three months as if I were in a treatment center. What do you think?

That is an excellent plan that you have, and as you say it is very intense. The problem is that it is "your" plan and depends on what you do to get free. And the reason that no plan will work is that it has already been done. You are already "dead to sin and freed from it". You have been crucified with Christ and you no longer live, but Christ lives in you. You have it all. There is nothing more to do, but believe the truth of who you are in Christ and that Christ is your life and you are one spirit with him. As Martin Luther said over 500 years ago, "Nothing we do helps us spiritually". I, like you over the eight years I struggled with addiction, had many very spiritual and very intensive plans and I failed miserably to follow through on any of them. If you will take a look at my testimony in the introduction of how I found my freedom you will see that I tried 32 different things and all any of them did was to get me deeper into bondage. Why? Were they wrong things to do? No, they were all good things to do, but the problem was that I was doing them in the flesh depending on what I did, just as everyone who has a plan is doing. I needed to know and believe that apart from Christ I could do nothing and come to the end of myself and my resources. When I finally got to that point I was able to believe and receive the truth that Christ had set me free and He was living His life in me. That truth has kept me free from addiction for 32 years. I'm not telling you to not do any of these things, but I am telling you that if you depend on them and what you do instead of what Christ has done for you and who He is in you, that you will fail miserably. Also, I must point out that accountability is a joke and a farce. No one can hold you accountable for your actions. I know as I had a group of five godly and very mature Christians who tried it with me. It does not work. It is just another way for us to put ourselves under the law, just as we put ourselves under the law with our spiritual and intensive plans. I would suggest that you find someone to hold you accountable to believing the truth that sets you free and who you are in Christ instead of holding you accountable for your behavior, which is nothing but holding you accountable to the law.

*How can I know the will of God? If I can figure it out, then I
believe it would enable me to live in freedom and victory.*

This is another issue that you can't determine or figure it
out. But the good news is that you don't have to. You are
the will of God. The will of God is in you. Christ lives in
you and you no longer live and the life you now live, you
live by the faith of the Son of God. Here again it is so simple
that most miss it and are trying to figure out the will of
God by reason, logic, study, prayer, etc. In practical terms,
how does it work? You believe that you were crucified with
Christ and you no longer live, but Christ is living in you.
And you trust Christ as your life (Col. 3:4), knowing you are
One Spirit with Him (1 Cor. 6:17). The major problem with
most Christians is they believe Christ is separate from them
and spend their time trying to get closer to Him, and the
truth is they can't get any closer. He lives in them. Most are
spending their time doing their best to live the Christian life
by stopping sin, avoiding wrong, doing right, etc., but there
is only one Christian life, and that is Christ's life and He
lives in you. When we believe, that is when we get free from
all enslaving addictions and begin living in the peace, joy,
freedom and victory that Christ died on the cross to give us.

*Christianity Today has reported that virtually all Christian
recovery ministries are based on the 12 Steps. Why is this?*

The reason is that very few Christians (churches, pastors,
counselors, authors) understand the problem of addiction
and also the answer for addiction. They do not understand
that addiction is spiritual bondage and demands a spiritual

answer. One of the major reasons for this is that so very few have had any success in working with addicts and alcoholics. Relapse is so common and the things they tell the addict to do, which have seemed to have some sort of success with those who are not struggling with a major addiction, just do not bring any results. So basically, most of them have just given up and told them to go to AA and work the Steps and if that is not enough, they send them to a secular treatment center. I know as that is what happened to me. My home church which most believed was the most successful evangelical Church in the state told me to go to AA and then sent me to a secular treatment center. And when that didn't work, they started a Christian recovery ministry based on the 12 steps, which didn't work either. It is not that the 12 Steps are bad or wrong. If people will work them conscientiously, it will improve the quality of their life and possibly help them stop drinking and drugging temporarily, but it will not set them free. Freedom from addiction is only available through the person and the finished work of Christ. Christian recovery ministries make the same mistake the secular recovery programs do. They tell people what to do to change their behavior. Behavior modification has never worked and never will because that is not the problem. The problem is the false identity in the flesh that causes them to behave as they do. The answer for the Christian is to know who he is in Christ. It is to know that the old self was crucified with Christ and is no more (Gal. 2:20), that Christ is their life (Col. 3:4) and they are dead to sin and freed from it (Rom. 6:6, 7) and they are one with Christ (1 Cor. 6:17). There is nothing to do as it has already been done. Of course this answer is often not received well, as most are looking for something to do. And some think that is too simple or easy to just believe the truth. I agree that it is simple, but it is far from easy. In a way one of the most difficult things a Christian will ever do is believe the truth that "they have been crucified with Christ and they no longer live but Christ is living in them" (Gal. 2.20) and

"Christ is their life" (Col. 3:4) and "they are dead to sin and freed from it" Rom. 6:6,7). But belief in that truth is what makes you "really free" (John 8:36).

5|8

I went through your webinars several times. It's been about a year and a half, and it's truly amazing that I'm free. What chaps me the most though is I've been free for 30 years and just didn't know it. One thing I found was that after I received the revelation that I died and that I no longer live but Christ is my life, I would try to live in the sensation of that revelation. This feeling would slowly pass and I found myself doubting who I really was in Christ. It took some time, but I don't need to feel free. I am free. That was the turning point. You will know the truth and the truth will set you free. It's that word "know" that was key for me. Thank you, Mike.

Yes, Jesus said, "Then you will know the truth and the truth will set you free" (John 8:32). But probably about 90% of Christians are not experiencing their freedom as they are trying to get their feelings to line up with the truth of what God says, which will never happen. Yes, I believe you have nailed it. Feelings do not last and never will. I believe that is the main reason most Christians do not experience their freedom after they have learned the truth of it, or rather have the information or knowledge. I have never felt "I was free" on a consistent basis. But the truth is I am free because my old self was crucified with Christ and I no longer live, but Christ is living in me (Gal. 2:20). There are a lot of Christians that claim to "know" the truth, but because their feelings do not confirm it, they do not experience the "truth that sets free". By the way, don't let it bother you that it took 30 years. I was 51 years old and had been a Christian for 18 years before I experienced my freedom in Christ 32 years ago. It takes what it takes to bring us to the point of brokenness and desperation. Desperation is the key to revelation, and no one experiences their freedom in Christ until they have completely given up on themselves and their resources. When that happens then and only then can we receive the truth that sets free. No need to worry that it took so long to experience your freedom as God uses everything in our lives for our good (Rom. 8:28). I suppose I could be upset over how long it took me to learn the truth, but God uses and works everything in our life for good. I wouldn't have the ministry and the marriage I have today without going through what I did. I'm certain that God will show you how He is using all those years that you went through for good in your life.

You talk often about Romans 6:14, "we are not under law, but under grace". I totally agree. What do you do then with all the commands Paul gives in that same book (especially chapters 12-15) and at the end of most of his epistles? Do you see a difference between these commands and law?

The big difference is that you have died to the law (Rom. 7:4) and are no longer under law but under grace (Rom. 7:14) As you said, we are not under law, but under grace. I believe that one of the things that means is that it is no longer up to us to do right, stop sinning and obey the law. We can trust Christ as our life (Col. 3:4). All of Paul's commands are directed to born again believers who have died to the law and have been released from it (Rom.7:4, 6). "We know that the law is good if one uses it properly. We also know that law is made not for the righteous but for lawbreakers and rebels, the ungodly and sinful, the unholy and irreligious; for those who kill their fathers or mothers, for murderers, for adulterers and perverts, for slave traders and liars and perjurers — and for whatever else is contrary to the sound doctrine" (1 Tim. 1:8–10). I see what you see as commands as actually exhortations addressed to us basically saying "Act like who you are, you are the righteousness of God. Don't you know who you are"? As Martin Luther said, the law has nothing to say to a believer. He also said, "The law says do this and never is it done. Grace says believe in this One and it is already done". Watchman Nee said, "The law-keeper lives in us". It all gets us back to the fact that as a result of the finished work of Christ we are under a new covenant, "This is the covenant I will make with the house of Israel after that time, declares the Lord. I will put my laws in their minds and write them on their hearts. I will be their God, and they will be my people." (Heb.8:10). When we finally believe that we are not under law, but under grace and know who we are in Christ is when we will experience the freedom that has been provided for us.

On your last email, you said nothing to do to maintain? Apparently, I believed on March 31 and experienced my freedom. As I have said before I have experienced my freedom many times, but it does not last. How did your freedom last and mine always wither away? Why am I struggling to BELIEVE again? What happened to the believing faith I exercised on March 31? Did I stop believing? If so, how do I start back believing? Why am I only experiencing the same old, same old life as usual? What happened to the victory, the peace, the joy? I have been listening again and again to the webinars and you and Vernon keep saying only believe. How do I keep on believing? What is pulling me off the believing? When you found your freedom, did you ever lose it, regain it, lose it again? If not, what's wrong with my believing?

No, I have never lost my freedom and you haven't either. When you received Christ, you received freedom. Christ is your life (Col. 3:4) and your freedom (Gal. 5:1). I believe a big part of your problem is that you believe it is up to you to maintain, find, and keep your freedom. But that is a lie from the pit of hell. As Jesus said IT IS FINISHED! (JOHN 19:30). Your freedom is a done deal. There is nothing for you to do or not do. It has been done. The fact that you think there is something for you to do indicates you do not believe the truth of the finished work of Christ. You said that you experienced your freedom, but it did not last. The truth is that your freedom does not come and go. Every person in Christ is free, no matter what they are experiencing or not experiencing. In my first eighteen years as a Christian I did not experience my freedom, but I was as free as I am now. I believe that you think you are experiencing freedom when your emotions line up with the truth and you feel free. But you are as free now as you will ever be. Your problem is the same as with most Christians. You are trying to get your emotions to line up with the truth and that will never happen. Emotions come and go, but who you are in Christ and what you have in Christ never changes. STOP looking at your feelings and believe what God's word clearly says to you, that it was for freedom that Christ set you free (Gal. 5:1). It is a done deal, no matter what you do or don't do or how you feel. I have never felt free consistently. In fact, most of the times I don't feel free. But so, what? I am free regardless of how I feel. I have a plaque in my office that says "Truth is what God says, regardless of how I feel". AMEN! Your freedom does not depend on your emotions or how you feel. If it did depend on our feelings, no one would be experiencing freedom. You say "I don't know what am I doing wrong?" What you are doing wrong is anything you are trying to do to get, attain or obtain what Jesus has already given you. Instead of trying to do things why don't you thank and praise God for who you are (Christ as life in you) and what He has given you (freedom, peace, joy and victory). Every morning I thank God that I have been put to death on the cross with Christ; still I am living; no longer I, but Christ is living in me; and that life which I now am living in the flesh I am living by faith, the faith of the Son of God, who in love for me, gave himself up for me (Gal. 2:20 BBE). I also thank God that I am His beloved, blood-bought, born-again, blessed son/daughter on whom His favor rests and with whom He is well pleased and on whom there is no condemnation, guilt, shame, punishment, judgment, sin, death or hell (Rom 8:2) because Jesus is in the Father and I am in Jesus and Jesus is in me (John 14:20). What else could we possibly need or do? IT IS FINISHED!!!

61

Do you ever experience fear, anxiety, worry, stress? If so, what do you do when it comes to you?

Of course, I do. I am human and have all the emotional responses just like everyone else. Everyone on the face of the earth experiences fear, anxiety, worry and stress. But these are just emotional responses to the daily problems and issues we face. In the Big Book that most people in AA are reading, they say HALT, which is the acronym for "Don't get hungry, angry, lonely or tired". The problem is, we cannot control our emotional responses. For example, if a drunk driver runs me off the road into a ditch, I believe I would feel fear at first and then be very angry as I sat in the ditch in my car. We cannot control our emotional responses. The issue is what do we do with them. Our emotions very seldom tell us the truth. I do not have to let my emotions define who I am and determine how I act. I need to remember who I am in Christ and what I have in Christ. That doesn't mean I'm suddenly overflowing with peace and joy. But if I am believing the truth, then eventually my emotions will follow. It will probably take some time for the emotions to line up, and they probably never will completely. We are emotional beings and the emotions are just below the surface and can break out at any time. Jesus lived in a human body and experienced all the emotions that we do and all the temptations that we do. He got hungry (Luke 4:2), angry (John 2:15) tired (John 4:6) and was under considerable stress before His crucifixion (Luke 22:44). I think He also felt lonely as He cried out on the cross, "My God, my God, why have you forsaken me?" (Matt. 27:46), but His Father was in Him and He was in constant contact and communication with Him. "…you will leave me all alone. Yet I am not alone, for my Father is with me" (John 16:32). By the way, Christ lives in us and nothing can stop us from being in contact and communication with Him. Most of the time we do not feel as Christ is living in us and is our life, but as I said our emotions very seldom tell us the truth. AND it is the "truth that sets us free."

A gracious thank you for the 3 disk CD Freedom From Addictive Behaviors. You have even personally replied to my emails. I can't even tell you how much that has impacted me. I'm still smoking heroin but I think I'm afraid because after I go to a medical detox for 5 or 7 days I'm great and the withdrawals are gone. Hard part done. But what if my wanting to use again is greater than my wanting to be free? Or sober, in other words. I'm telling you it's gonna take a miracle for MY mind to NOT want to smoke heroin.

You said it would take a miracle for your mind to not want to smoke heroin. The Good News is that the miracle has taken place as Gal. 2:20 tells us, and "since, then, you have been raised with Christ, set your hearts on things above, where Christ is seated at the right hand of God. Set your minds on things above, not on earthly things. For you died, and your life is now hidden with Christ in God. When Christ, who is your life, appears, then you also will appear with him in glory" (Col. 3:1-4). Practically everyone struggling with an addictive behavior is focusing on, and trying to change, their behavior, which is absolutely the wrong thing to do. Behavior modification does not work. God solved our problems not by showing us what to do by improving ourselves so we wouldn't do the behavior but by putting to death the old sinner selves that we were and making us a new creation (2 Cor. 5:17), who is dead to sin and freed from it (Rom. 6:6, 7). The simple, startling and stunning truth is that when we know who we are in Christ and what we have in Him is when we experience freedom from addiction. You will probably want to use again and feel like that is greater than your desire to be free. BUT YOU NEED TO REALIZE THAT IT IS BASED ON A DECEPTION! IT IS A LIE! The feeling is very real and seems to be overpowering, but it is not the truth. It is just a feeling and feelings usually do not tell you the truth. The feeling is like the ones we have when we feel angry or overcome with lust. The answer to it is to believe the truth of who you are in Christ. The answer to a lie is always the truth. Jesus said, "Then you will know the truth and the truth will set you free" (John 8:32). This is where most Christians lose the battle. They are trying to get their feelings to line up with the truth and that will never happen. By the way, the lie is almost always based on the deception about who you are, your identity. When we believe Gal. 2:20 that "I have been crucified with Christ. It is no longer I who live, but Christ who lives in me. And the life I now live in the flesh I live by faith in the Son of God, who loved me and gave himself for me." (Gal. 2:20 ESV) and live in that truth is when we live free. Our behavior will not be perfect. I learned this truth 32 years ago and my behavior has certainly not been perfect, but I have been free from addiction all these years. Feelings are very powerful and they are real, but they do not tell you the truth. The truth is you are dead to sin and freed from it

(Rom. 6:6, 7) and Christ is your life (Col. 3:4) and you are one spirit with Him (1 Cor. 6:17). I know you don't feel like it and I don't either, but so what, it is the truth! The best thing you can do is to realize that you can't improve yourself, stop sinning and avoid wrong, but you do not have to do that. One of the major mistakes we make is in believing that Christ is apart from us and we need to pray and beg Him to change us and help us do right. He has changed us and He is not apart from us. He is our life and is living in us and when we know and believe that is when we live free. Since Christ is your life and is living in you, then you have the mind of Christ (1 Corin. 2:16). What do you need to do? As Jesus told Jairus the synagogue ruler who had been told "your daughter is dead…why bother the teacher anymore?", "Don't be afraid, just believe." (Mark 5:35-36).

Why do addicts lie and manipulate others?

When I was in a Christian treatment center, the Director would say "All addicts are liars. Not all liars are addicts, but all addicts are liars". He was right. They do not tell the truth and they manipulate others. I know as I struggled with alcoholism for eight years and that is what I did. I have been free from my addiction for 32 years and have been in a recovery ministry for that time and have witnessed many examples of this. The reason addicts do not tell the truth is that they do not want help. Well, actually they want to deal with their issue and learn to cope and stay out of trouble, but they do not want to change as a person. If they did, they could get help as there is extensive help available (secular and Christian). I have a list of over 100 Christian treatment centers and there are hundreds of secular treatment centers. I have a list of at least 100 Christian counselors in the U.S. and there are many more secular counselors. The reality is that those struggling with an addictive behavior do not want to come to grips with the reality that they cannot deal with their problem. They will fight and struggle with every fiber of their body to not give up and come to the end of themselves and their resources. BUT until they reach that point, they will not be able to turn to God and find His answer of freedom in Christ. I never tell anyone what to do as that is between them and God. You just need to act in faith, trusting God. However, I believe you are doing the right thing and truthfully it is the best thing you can do for him is to separate yourself from him. The most loving and redemptive thing my wife did for me during my alcoholism was kick me out of the house. I was forced to attend a Christian treatment center. I would counsel you to make sure you forgive him and keep on forgiving him. But as I say in Chapter 8 in my book, "Helping Others Overcome Addictions", you should "speak the truth in love and exercise tough love". You might want to read Chapter 8 again. Keep in mind that you should not take actions to try to get him to change or do anything, but simply because it is the right thing to do and you are acting in faith and trusting God.

My husband is an unbeliever and has absolutely no interest in God. He is also an alcoholic and has zero interest in quitting. Is it possible to live in love with an unbeliever?

Yes, it is possible to live in love with an unbeliever. In fact, to live in love with them is really the only way you can really live with them. In fact, it is the only way you live with a believer or an unbeliever! My marriage of 45 years is a testament to that. If we try to do it out of duty, responsibility or even trying to keep the marriage covenant we will fail totally and completely. You can live in love with them because God (Christ) is love, and He lives in you. The fruit of the Spirit is love, and as you live by faith in the Spirit, it will happen. You may never have good, romantic and sympathetic feelings of love, but even if you did, they wouldn't last. Your question can also be asked if it is possible to live in love with anyone (believers or unbelievers). Believe me, I know. My wife and I have been married 45 years and we would not be together today without love that has nothing to do with good feelings. As you know I struggled with alcoholism for eight years and I was a Christian but not acting as one. Forgiveness is essential, not just for that, but the only way that two people can live together in love. One of the main issues here is that "from now on, therefore, we regard no one according to the flesh. Even though we once regarded Christ according to the flesh, we regard him thus no longer" (2 Cor. 5:16). That is not just for an unbeliever, but absolutely essential for everyone (all believers included). Too many times we all get in the flesh and act like the devil. You really cannot live in love in your own self-effort, that is in your own strength, wisdom and love because we don't have any. But Christ in you who is love is your life and He can and will do it through you, in you and as you. Check out this poem below. SEE-THROUGHER by Darrell Scott

A wise old man once said to me
"Don't trust the things your eyes can see
'Cause if you do you'll know confusion
Always judging, by illusion"

"Don't look at _____; see through, my friend
Beyond the frown, the sneer, the grin
Peer deep into the living soul
Where beauty, wonders will unfold

Both fear and judgment fall apart
When viewing others from the heart
So don't look at, adjust your view
And focus deeper, seeing through!

(Darrell Scott wrote the above about our friend Norman Grubb. Norman had a profound effect on his life before tragedy struck. Darrell's daughter was one of the first murdered in the Columbine school shooting. Since that time, Darrell has traveled all over speaking to groups, telling them how seeing through to the purposes of God in that tragedy brought him into God's rest and peace).

Do you think there is any value in going to school to be Christian counselor or a pastor or a Christian family therapist? If identity is key...what about finding financial provision and a job you like? Is that part of freedom in Christ?

Yes, there is value in going to school. I spent three years going to a seminary which I thought would prepare me to be a pastor. It did not. But the degree I earned enabled me to secure a position. The reason "identity is key" is that until we know who we are in Christ and that Christ is our life and we no longer live, but Christ lives in us and we now live by faith (Gal. 2:20) we will be trying to live the Christian life in our own strength and resources (flesh). We will be trying to avoid sin, get free, mature, be sanctified (in the flesh), which is doomed to failure. But God uses all of that to bring us to the end of ourselves so that we will finally give up on self and turn to Christ and trust him to be our life, which He is (Col. 3:4). When we know and believe that is when we experience peace, joy, freedom and fulfillment regardless of our position, situation, circumstances, job, ministry, relationships, family, etc., etc. But in answer to your second question, no finding financial provision and a job you like is not part of freedom in Christ. Freedom in Christ has been provided through the finished work of Christ. And when we know that our old self has been crucified with Christ and we no longer live but Christ lives in us and we live by faith in that truth is when we know "the truth that sets free", which is that we are dead to in and freed from it (Rom. 6:6, 7). Every Christian is already "free in Christ" but it seems most of them don't believe they are. So regardless of their occupation or lack of one, every Christian has the same opportunity to experience "freedom in Christ."

How would you get involved in professional ministry? Or just avoid that all together?

No, I certainly wouldn't avoid ministry and I have not done that. I have spent 40 years in full-time ministry. As to how I would get involved in ministry, I remember the advice given to me by some wise men - "Don't go into ministry unless that is all you can do." In other words, don't go into ministry unless the Lord has called you to it. Follow your heart, but let God direct you. I think God leads us to where He wants us. That doesn't mean there will not be some starts and stops and even some backing up. There certainly was with me. Initially, I was planning on being a pastor, but that was not where God wanted me, so after my first eight years of ministry and then eight years of struggling with addiction, God called me to this ministry of helping people find freedom from addiction. This was not the ministry I would have chosen. I chose to be a pastor, but I know now this is what I should be doing and cannot imagine doing anything else and I am fulfilled in it. I believe the three basics you need to go into ministry is 1) An understanding and love and acceptance of those struggling with addictions or whatever. 2) Know and believe the truth that sets free (that we are dead to sin and dead to the law). Knowing you are dead to sin is your union and identity with Christ and knowing and believing you are dead to the law is an understanding of grace) 3) A call from God. How do you know if you have a call from God? "Don't go into ministry unless that is all you can do."

You have shared that your ministry has not been well received and that many do not respond to it. How do you feel about that?

I believe that what my ministry does is present the truth that sets free. And a big part of that is to know and believe that Christ is your life. And to receive and believe truth there must be a revelation of that truth that only can come from God. My ministry is simply to share that truth and trust God to give the revelation of "the truth that sets free." Before a person can receive this truth, they must come to the end of self and know there is absolutely nothing they can do to get free. Usually that is a long and painful process. As the apostle Paul put it, "We do not want you to be uninformed, brothers, about the hardships we suffered in the province of Asia. We were under great pressure, far beyond our ability to endure, so that we despaired even of life. Indeed, in our hearts we felt the sentence of death. But this happened that we might not rely on ourselves but on God, who raises the dead." (2 Cor. 1:8–9). Desperation is always the key to revelation. Do I get discouraged at times? Yes, but I am encouraged by Ezekiel when God called him into ministry and told him, "The people to whom I am sending you are obstinate and stubborn. Say to them, 'This is what the Sovereign LORD says.' And whether they listen or fail to listen — for they are a rebellious house — they will know that a prophet has been among them."(Ezek. 2:4–5). And also by Isaiah "Go and tell this people: 'Be ever hearing, but never understanding; be ever seeing, but never perceiving'...Then I said, 'For how long, O Lord?' And he answered: 'Until the cities lie ruined and without inhabitant, until the houses are left deserted and the fields ruined and ravaged'" (Isa. 6:9, 11). In the final analysis, there are thousands of ways people are told what to do to cope with addiction, but there is only one way they can find freedom from addiction and that is through the finished work of Christ. There is no other way. But it is available to all who stop relying on self and rely on God who raises the dead. As I have said, I am not a fan of AA but they do a good job of what their purpose is and that is giving people things to do to cope with their addiction. My main problem is that they don't point people to Christ and his finished work, but they are not trying to do that. One of their sayings I agree with is "It takes what it takes." What does it take? It takes coming to the end of self and your resources.

I have watched all your webinars and read your material. I agree with everything you teach. Unfortunately, I am still bound in overeating. I'm not sure why I am not finding freedom. Do you have any testimonies of people being freed from an addiction to overeating?

There have been people freed from an addiction to overeating, but I don't have any names. I'm going to send out an announcement for an upcoming webinar and will ask if anyone has been freed and see if I get any responses and if I do, I will let you know. Keep in mind that (1) Freedom has been provided through the finished work of Christ and that is the only way anyone experiences freedom (See Gal. 5:1 and Gal. 2:20). (2) How does one experience it? It is always and only by faith in the truth. It is not enough to have the knowledge or information. As Romans 10 says, "The word is near you; it is in your mouth and in your heart," that is, the word of faith we are proclaiming: That if you confess with your mouth, "Jesus is Lord," and believe in your heart that God raised him from the dead, you will be saved. For it is with your heart that you believe and are justified, and it is with your mouth that you confess and are saved." (Rom. 10:8, 9, 10). (3) The two primary reasons most don't believe and are not free is that they are striving to get their feelings to line up with the truth which will never happen and/or they have not come to the end of self and totally given up on anything they can do to get free. You cannot trust Christ as your life until you give up on your life. The apostle Paul puts it like this. We do not want you to be uninformed, brothers, about the hardships we suffered in the province of Asia. We were under great pressure, far beyond our ability to endure, so that we despaired even of life. Indeed, in our hearts we felt the sentence of death. But this happened that we might not rely on ourselves but on God, who raises the dead. (2 Cor. 1:8, 9).

Thank you so very much for your testimony and hard work in putting these webinars together. You guys do a wonderful job. Unfortunately, I still have the chains of alcohol pulling me down in a deep dark pit. I have no self-control in this area. Over 10 years of continuous up and down, start and stop. I have a job and family and manage to survive but am sick of this lifestyle. My wife has no idea about this ongoing struggle. She helped me through this a few years ago, but I started drinking again and now it seems to be my best friend/worse enemy. "As a dog returns to his vomit...". Thank you for letting me share this with you. In fact, you are the only one I have shared this with in many years.?

Thanks for sharing with me. I have some good news for you. In fact, it is so good that most think it is too good to be true.

The good news is that no one on the face of this earth has self-control. Not me, you or anybody. But the best part of this good news is that you don't need any. Self-control lives in you in the life of Jesus. As you believe this truth and give up on yourself and realize that there is absolutely nothing you can do to break the bondage of addiction and learn to trust Christ as your life, you will break this bondage. The truth is, you are already free as Gal. 2:20, Gal. 5:1 and Rom. 6:6, 7 and many other verses tell us. But as long as you or anyone is trying to quit and/or exercise self-control, it will not happen. One of the most liberating lessons I ever learned was that I can't get my act together. I can't stop sinning, do right, avoid wrong or do anything good, loving and redemptive. In other words, I cannot live the Christian life, but then I don't have to. There is only one Christian life, and that is the life of Christ who is your life (Col. 3:4). We live by faith, not by feelings, sight, circumstances, or what anyone else says (no matter what their credentials are), etc. I realize that the majority of Christians do not believe this, but so what? It is the "truth that sets you free" (John 8:32). If you will send me your regular mailing address, I will send you a copy of our latest book, "Helping Others Overcome Addictions". The title is somewhat misleading as the first seven chapters get into what the problem of addiction is, why it is so hard to get free from, and God's clear, complete and definitive answer for addiction. I believe the key verse to get free is Gal. 2:20, "I have been put to death on the cross with Christ; still I am living; no longer I, but Christ is living in me; and that life which I now am living in the flesh I am living by faith, the faith of the Son of God, who in love for me, gave himself up for me". The reason it is key is 1) It says the old self that you were is dead and gone. You cannot shape up a dead person. The alcoholic self that you were is no more. 2) The life you are living now is Christ in you. And now you are living by faith, the faith of the Son of God. 3) Jesus is living in you and is your life and when you know and believe this earth shattering, mind blowing truth is when you begin to walk and live free.

I have been thinking about your request to hear from people set free from overeating and trying to decide whether or not to respond. I would love to talk with you about it. My hesitation is that even after 20-plus years of involvement and teaching about freedom in Christ and experiencing significant freedom in other areas of my life, this one continued to plague me. 15 years ago I found freedom from this bondage for a year and a half. I even called and talked with you about it at that time because I had questions. But then I lost it. I have very recently been experiencing significant freedom again from overeating, but because of past experience have not shared about it. I know this freedom is available long term and hope to share more about the victory. Both times it has been a new understanding and BELIEF IN particular verses from Romans 6 that impacted me. I know that's no surprise. This time 6:11 "...consider yourselves..."! I guess I didn't quite believe ..."I can! ...because...".

Keep in mind that "You are free", no matter how you are feeling, what you have done or what you are doing. You cannot lose it. I very seldom feel free and even when I do it does not last very long. But my feelings do not tell me the truth. We all live in a fallen, fleshly body and we will continue to have ungodly and fleshly desires. We still have all of our flesh patterns in our brains and will have them until we go to be with the Lord. There is no hope or possibility of clearing that up or changing them. But of course, that is not who you are. The answer for every lie is faith in the truth that Christ is your life (Col. 3:4), that you are dead to sin and freed from it (Rom. 6:6, 7). You cannot get any freer than you are now. Of course, as you believe the "truth that sets you free" (John 8:32) you will begin to live in it and experience it. I have been a Christian for 50 years and I have been free from addiction for 32 years, but my emotions often do not line up with the truth. But so, what? The truth is I have been crucified with Christ and I no longer live, but Christ lives in me. The life I live in the body, I live by faith in the Son of God, who loved me and gave himself for me. (Gal. 2:20). Truth is what God says, regardless of my feelings! I think you struggle with the same thing that all of us do, and that is your emotions do not measure up with the truth and never will. We believe and have faith in our heart as Rom. 10:4, 5 tell us, "The word is near you; it is in your mouth and in your heart," that is, the word of faith we are proclaiming: That if you confess with your mouth, "Jesus is Lord," and believe in your heart that God raised him from the dead, you will be saved". Heart is Spirit and where we believe truth.

71

My youngest son is finishing up a year program at Teen Challenge. Our middle son went through a similar struggle six or seven years ago. The ripple effect of all of this is that I still struggle not to enable him (not financially, not with school, but in other ways) - because I want him to be better. And I do feel responsible for much of his problems with addiction for a number of reasons. My husband can attest that I didn't want him to struggle in school, so I took on his issues all the time. I was pretty much a helicopter parent who wanted to fix every problem, make things better, and make up for the time spent away from him at work, with his brothers - etc. And my biggest fear that I am still hanging on to is - what if he relapses and leaves and we never see him again. I know it sounds crazy to be afraid of what hasn't happened. So, the thing is - other people notice this (especially his older brother) - who told me yesterday that he doesn't even like talking to me about his brother

*because it feels like my whole life is centered around what
he does and doesn't do. And my husband agreed I struggle
with this. He said - "the things you do, you listen to their
sermons, you listen to their music - just to feel like you
are a part of what he is doing." So, I guess I need to re-
read your book, because even though it is my son with
the "addiction problem" that you can see, I have had and
have a different problem. I am addicted to being the "fixer
mom". Only - when I do this, I am not seeing that the result
is pushing people I love further and further away. And the
person I am trying to "fix" also is uncomfortable by it all.
The thoughts of "see it's your fault he has these problems"
--- continue to attack my thinking - even though I know
the truth of the Gospel. And shame and blame are never a
helpful, productive thing. The "what ifs" are so frustrating
to deal with. So, before I can be a good helper to anyone
overcoming addiction, my prayer is that the Lord shows me
my real problem. That He works in the garden of my heart
and uproots those things I have been struggling with and
hanging onto. Things that keep me from fully living in the
free abundant life that is mine daily in Jesus Christ. I do not
want to be that enabler mom any longer. I want to rest in
grace, truth and peace.*

I believe the Lord has shown you what your real problem
is. If you will just look at your email to me it seems that
you have clearly pinpointed the problem. You said that
you are "addicted to being a fixer Mom". You need to
realize that is what codependency is. Codependency is an
addiction as much as an addiction to drugs, sex or alcohol.
Basically, codependency is when you are dependent on what
someone else does or says for your acceptance and worth.
The codependent is dependent on another person's actions
and responses for their own identity. The truth is that the
way we find acceptance and worth is how we find life. And
how we find life is how we find our identity. (1) First, let's
just start at the beginning and work through what you have

said in your email. You said that you want him to do better and you feel responsible for much of his actions. We are not responsible for anyone's actions. One of the most valuable lessons I learned as a pastor was that it was not my ministry to make anyone do anything and/or fix them. The truth is that when we try to fix anyone, they will instinctively rebel against what we are trying to do. As Neil Anderson used to say, "People don't care what you know until they know that you care". Trying to fix someone is a not-so-subtle form of rejection. It says to them that "you do not accept they the way they are so they need to change so you will accept them". People do not respond to that message of rejection. (2) As your older son told you, "your whole life is centered around what he does and doesn't do." As long as you continue to do this it is guaranteed to result in misery. What should you do? You need to come to grips with reality that your son is in God's hands, and more importantly you are as well. Your deliverance from this addiction will come just like anyone's no matter what the addiction. When you know and believe that your life has been crucified with Christ and you no longer live, but Christ lives in you and you now live by faith in the One who loved you and gave Himself for you (Gal. 2:20) is when you will be freed from your addiction to codependency. That is the only way anyone gets free from any bondage and all addiction is spiritual bondage. When we believe that we are new creations (2Cor. 5:17) and that Christ is our life (Col. 3:4) and that we are dead to sin and freed from it (Rom. 6:6, 7) is when we find our freedom that has already been provided for us. The greatest and most liberating truth we can learn is that "Christ is in you" and we are one with Christ (1 Cor. 3:17) and that is when we come into rest and STOP DOING AND TRYING to live the Christian life, get free, fix anyone, improve ourselves, do better, stop sinning, etc., etc.

72

I was looking up a quote from last week's webinar from Martin Luther. Do you gather that this gent has "rewritten" Luther's Galatians introduction in an accurate manner?

Dr. C. John (Jack) Miller, would often give strugglers the assignment to re-write Luther's Introduction to Galatians in their own words. Bill Slack's response to Jack Miller's assignment eventually made its way into the Sonship discipleship materials.

The short answer to your question is "Yes, I believe he has rewritten Luther's Galatians introduction accurately. I have read that rewritten introduction many times. I attended a Sonship conference and am very familiar with the Sonship materials. I knew Jack Miller, his wife Rosemary and their son Paul. Some of the first teaching on grace I received were Jack Miller's tapes on Galatians. All of this was before I experienced my freedom from addiction. When I experienced my freedom, I wrote to Jack Miller and told him that whereas I greatly appreciated what I had learned from him about grace and that I was dead to the law I did not experience freedom until I learned that I was "dead to sin and freed from it" (Rom. 6:6, 7). I now know that for a person to experience their freedom they must know they are (1) Dead to the law, an understanding of grace that frees them to live free and (2) Dead to sin as Christ is their life and that is their identity. What does that mean? It means their identity in Christ. It means that no one experiences true freedom in Christ until they know who they are and what they have in Christ. I am a great admirer of Luther and have read his commentary on Galatians and greatly benefited from it. It is lengthy and wordy, but is full of many spiritual gems. However, Luther doesn't write about our identity in Christ and in Slack's rewritten introduction says, "I am indeed a sinner". I believe Luther has a good understanding of grace as anyone and much better than most, and I read his Daily Devotional "By Faith Alone" every day. Luther was the primary driving force of the Reformation and the main book he camped out on was Galatians. All evangelical protestants owe him a great deal.

73

Obviously, clinical addictions to drugs, porn, alcohol, etc., are powerful deterrents to the abundant life Jesus promised. It's just that when those addictions are the focus, it plays into the con that all the other people who aren't terrorized by those addictions are somehow free. Satan has duped the whole world and almost 100% of so-called Christians that they are all addicted (bound) to their flesh. I wish you guys would broaden your focus and help break this con that is being perpetrated on all men.

If you have read any of our books or attended any of our webinars, you will know that we teach it is our belief only about 10% of Christians are experiencing their freedom in Christ, and of the 90%, many are not addicted to drugs, sex and alcohol. Satan is very creative and there are many addictions (addictive behaviors) that are robbing Christians of their freedom in Christ such as perfectionism, gambling, workaholism, anorexia, bulimia, homosexuality, performance-based acceptance, and materialism just to name a few. The primary reasons we emphasize drugs, sex and alcohol is (1) That was my personal struggle and (2) Those are people who know that they have a problem (though certainly not all of them) and are more open to hearing and believing the truth that sets free (3) That is primarily the ministry to which God has called me. The truth that we teach is THE TRUTH that sets anyone free. But I firmly believe that it takes a revelation from God for a person to believe "they are dead to sin and dead to the law." When a person knows who they are in Christ and what they have in Christ, that Christ is their life (Col. 3:4), that they are dead to sin and freed from it (Rom. 6:6, 7) is when they experience their freedom. But I have never seen anyone find their freedom until they experienced brokenness (coming to the end of self). Desperation opens the door to revelation! The truth that sums it up is "I have been crucified with Christ and I no longer live, but Christ lives in me. The life I live in the body, I live by faith in the Son of God, who loved me and gave himself for me." (Gal 2:20 NIV). When they believe that truth is when they walk free. No one gets free until they know the old self is crucified, dead and buried and is no more and they are a new creation and Christ is their life. There are many who have benefited from our ministry who have not had an addiction to drugs, alcohol or sex. Below is an email I received from someone today. "I have read your book (Helping Others Overcome Addictions) and gone through the webinar a couple years ago. I was required to read the book for Global Grace Seminary. This time reading through it was a whole new experience! My book is tattered from dog-earring and underlining! I now have an awareness of the utter beauty and magnificent love of Jesus like never before! Thanks for your work in aiding others to know the grace and love of God! I know I will utilize your materials as I practice Grace-Based Counseling. How blessed we are to live as Christ!"

This is rather a long question, but it gets right to the heart of the matter considering the problem and the answer for addiction. Mike, we have seen a number of men and women freed from addiction to drugs, porn, and alcohol here. We make sure that they know who they are in Christ and that they are no longer self-identified as addicts. Something came

up the other evening in a meeting. One of the people there said that a person who has come to Christ and knows the truth of who they are in Christ is no longer an addict. That addiction ceases. I tended to disagree in part. I was reading yours and Steve McVey's book "Helping Others Overcome Addictions" and I came across a quote from a lady who said this: "I was set free by understanding who I am in Christ....I told (my group) 'I am not an alcoholic by nature! I am a righteous child of God who has a physical and psychological vulnerability toward alcohol abuse, but that isn't what defines me.....'" (p. 133). My take on what she says and my understanding of what it means to be "in Christ" is that the person who is an abuser of drugs, alcohol, porn, etc. has little ability to refrain from that abusive addiction before accepting Christ; however, after coming to Jesus, the Holy Spirit works in them so that they do have the ability to refrain, but that they must "die daily" to any desire. The Holy Spirit empowers them to do so. My disagreement is that for some, perhaps many, going back to the source of the abuse (drugs, alcohol, etc.) may send them on a spiral back toward their own self-abuse from whence they came. In other words, because of that "physical and psychological vulnerability" their addiction can return. Therefore, a person, for example, who had an addiction to alcohol but has gained legitimate freedom in Christ cannot go into a bar with friends and have a couple of drinks without the strong possibility that he or she may return to the same behavior as experienced before coming to freedom. So would it be fair to say that someone had freedom from addiction, but because of being physically and psychologically vulnerable, they may be always subject to addiction if they return to the source?

I would have to agree with the person who said that "a person who has come to Christ and knows the truth of who they are in Christ is no longer an addict. That addiction ceases." That was my experience 32 years ago when I believed Gal. 2:20, "that my old self had been crucified with Christ and I no longer lived, but Christ was living in me" and was my life (Col. 3:4). But I had been a Christian 18 years at that point and was a seminary graduate and a former pastor. I had been struggling with an addiction to alcohol because I was believing a lie that I was an alcoholic (addict). I believe that most Christians are not experiencing their freedom in Christ because they believe what their experiences and emotions tell them instead of what God tells them. I have heard Neil Anderson say on many occasions that only 10% of Christians are experiencing freedom. Most are not struggling with an addiction to drugs, alcohol or sex, but there are many bondages such as perfectionism, codependency, materialism, etc. When I believed that Christ was my life and I was dead to sin and freed from it (Rom. 6:6, 7) I was freed from my addiction and have been for 32 years. I haven't lived a perfect life as my wife would confirm, but I have been free from addiction. You quoted the person who said, "I am a righteous child of God who has a physical and psychological vulnerability toward alcohol abuse, but that isn't what defines me.....' (p. 133). The psychological vulnerability toward alcohol is in our flesh and that is not who we are. We are not physical beings who have received a spirit. We are spiritual beings who live in a body. I often tell people that from time to time I feel insecure, inadequate, and inferior, but I know they are just feelings and they do not define who I am and do not determine my behavior. A big part of my ministry is I believe and teach that addiction is spiritual bondage. By that I mean that strongholds of addiction, etc. are developed as we attempt to meet our basic God-given needs of (1) love and acceptance and (2) worth and value in our own resources (our flesh) and/or turn to some things like alcohol, drugs, sex, etc., when they are not being met. I certainly did. Since addiction is spiritual bondage, THE ONLY ANSWER IS TO KNOW WHO YOU ARE IN CHRIST. When a person learns as I did that he is not insecure, inadequate, inferior and guilty but Christ is living in him as their life, they experience their freedom. Of course, it is a real stretch to believe that and only a small percentage of the people I'm telling that truth to believe it. But when they do, they are "free indeed" (John 8:32, 36). So, I do not believe that we "may be always subject to addiction if they return to the source?" For 32 years I have a beer (and sometimes two) or a glass of wine now and then and it is has not been an issue for me. I was at a Christmas party last night and had two glasses of wine, and the thought never crossed my mind to have another one. If Christ is our life and the old self was crucified with Him and we no longer live, but Christ is living in us and the life we live, we now live by faith in the Son of God who loved us and gave Himself for us" (Gal. 2:20), what else could we possibly need.

75

I wrote to you a couple of days ago, but I think I had a breakthrough yesterday where I am beginning to understand what you're saying about the old self being crucified with Christ. As I mentioned before, I have wrestled with depression and despair for many years, and I currently wake up during the night each night and a bolt of anxiety instantly surges through me. But last night I just kept saying, "That's not who I am. That old self that worries and fears and panics has been crucified with Christ. It is dead and powerless. I have been crucified with Christ, and it is no longer I who live, but Christ who lives in me." I said that over and over, and I had peace amidst the storm and went back to sleep faster than usual. I realized that I have spent a lot of time and energy trying to fix, control, or numb my sinful flesh, in an effort to get rid of sinful thoughts altogether. But I can't do that. Nothing works. I just have to accept that my sinful flesh exists on this earth and it will try hard to annoy and harass me, but my comfort and peace is in knowing, really knowing that it has been crucified and buried, and it is powerless. When I have irrational anxious thoughts or powerful feelings of sadness, those are from the part of me that has died and I can dismiss them as such. I have tried over and over to discipline myself to think positive thoughts, to be thankful, to ask for forgiveness, but nothing has seemed to work and I have plunged deeper and deeper into despair. I have tried various medications to try to numb myself or think more positively, but that either doesn't work or I just feel numb altogether. I think that is what you mean by trying to fix the sinful flesh. It can't be done. It is only when I accept the truth that I can't fix myself and that my sinful self has already died, that I can have peace through what Christ has done for me. I can't stop sinful thoughts from entering my brain or impulses from surging through my body, but I don't have to try to fix or eliminate them--that just makes things worse. Just believe the truth that they are not me; I am a new creation. I think this is applying the truths that you've taught, and I will continue thinking about them. Thank you for taking the time to explain the gospel and what it means for us. This is a new understanding for me.

YES, I believe you have had a breakthrough! It appears you are experiencing the truth of the first part of Gal. 2:20 that the old self that you were is crucified with Christ, dead, buried and is no more. And yes, we all do spend a lot of time trying to fix and control our flesh, but as you are seeing that is not who you are. And as you said, you cannot fix the flesh. That is one of the most liberating truths I have ever learned. I am 83 years old and I still find it discouraging that I have sinful thoughts and even behavior from time to time. But I have to remind myself that it is not who I am, just like you said. The flesh is never going to change. I feel insecure, inferior, inadequate and guilty from time to time, but I do not have to let those thoughts define who I am and determine how I act. As you said, "It is only when I accept the truth that I can't fix myself and that my sinful self has already died, that I can have peace through what Christ has done for me. I can't stop sinful thoughts from entering my brain or impulses from surging through my body, but I don't have to try to fix or eliminate them—that just makes things worse. Just believe the truth that they are not me; I am a new creation." That is the second part of Gal. 2:20 "that you no longer live but Christ is living in you and the life you now live, you live by the faith of the Son of God who loved you and gave Himself for you". Is it that simple? YES, IT IS! But it is not easy as we live in a fallen world in which Satan rules and your flesh never changes and Satan continually lies to you and accuses you. I experienced my freedom 32 years ago, but it hasn't gotten much easier for me. It is not easy because faith is believing what you don't see or feel and in an invisible ONE that you don't see. One final thought. Don't spend too much time thinking about it. Just know and believe that it is the truth regardless of what you see, feel or what anyone else says. In Mark 5:35, 36 when people came from Jairus house and told him, "Your daughter is dead, why bother the teacher anymore? ", Jesus told him, "Don't be afraid; just believe".

I'm still teaching the "Helping Others" course. Can you please clarify the statement on the last slide of part 5 that says anything is permissible? I understand that nothing we do can separate us from Christ, but how do I explain and clarify this particular statement better?

I'm just quoting Scripture 1 Corinthians 6:12 "'Everything is permissible for me,' but not everything is beneficial. 'Everything is permissible for me,' but I will not be mastered by anything" (CSB). 1 Corinthians 10:23 (NIV) "'I have the right to do anything,' you say—but not everything is beneficial. 'I have the right to do anything'—but not everything is constructive". The literal Greek word is "lawful". 1 Corinthians 10:23 (NASB) "All things are lawful, but not all things are profitable. All things are lawful, but not all things edify". Often when I don't quote the whole verse, the person will come back to me and say you need to use the verse in context that "all things are lawful, but not all things are profitable and beneficial". But to use scripture in its proper context, we must use it in the context of the finished work of Christ. So many will take a verse from the Old Testament or even in the New Testament and use it as if the cross and the resurrection never took place. Many will use scripture to prove their particular bias, but if it is not used in the context that (1) Sin has been taken care of and is no longer an issue (2) We are dead to the law redeemed from it and not under it (3) The old person that we were is dead and no more and we are dead to sin and freed from it (4) We are new creations (2 Cor. 5:17) and Christ is our life (Col. 3:4), that, I believe, is why we find so much legalism in the Church today. If we understand the new covenant and what the finished work of Christ accomplished, we will be amazed at the freedom, peace and joy it has provided for us. I think it will take an eternity to understand the grace of God in Christ. But that seems like a good way to spend time there with Jesus. Why would the Apostle Paul say that all things are lawful? I believe one of the reasons is that so few Christians understand the grace of God. The fact is that it seems that most Christian do not know they are dead to the law and as Martin Luther said "the law has nothing to say to the Christian." Rom. 6:14 says For sin shall not be your master, because you are not under law, but under grace. Rom. 7:4, 6 says So, my brothers, you also died to the law through the body of Christ, that you might belong to another, to him who was raised from the dead, in order that we might bear fruit to God. As I have said before there are two things you must absolutely know to be free. You must know you are dead to sin and Christ is your life, which is your identity. And you must know you are dead to the law, which is an understanding of grace.

77

I have had anxiety/depression/OCD for at least 25 years. My childhood involved emotional/sexual/mental abuse and a lot of neglect. Both parents expected perfection (and punished when I wasn't) and my mom often said, "what is wrong with you" and "you should be ashamed of yourself". I do not consciously blame them because I know they did the best they could. I've been to many counselors, prayer sessions, inner healings, etc, etc. and been a believer since I was 5 or 6 years old. I struggle with feeling guilty most of the time and have crazy high expectations of myself. I feel a lot of shame and, of course, think I should have all this together by now and be much closer to perfection than I am at this point. I am on medication now that prevents the dangerously high anxiety and dangerously low depression as I was very ready to end it all early this fall because I saw no hope of ever getting to the other side of this and/or ever really knowing the love of God. I have prayed at least a thousand times to know His love and feel like a child of His. I know ours is not supposed to be an experiential religion all the time, but I KNOW I am supposed to feel SOMETHING and certainly not feel like a guilty slave. Oh, I feel very often that I have to do this or that in order for God to help me be healed. Read this book, listen to this course, pray this prayer, be obedient in this, etc., etc.

Let's start with this you say "you KNOW you are supposed to feel something". But really you are feeling a lot of things, which is one of your major problems. You feel anxiety, depression, guilt and shame. Either one of those is enough to keep you in bondage and rob you of your freedom. I know as I struggled with all of those and still do from time to time. But I know that feelings do not tell you the truth. Now I know the truth that there is no more guilt and shame no matter what I or you do, as sin is no more. It was taken care of it on the cross. I believe that you are believing a lie from about who God is. 1 John 4:16 "And so we know and rely on the love God has for us. God is love. Whoever lives in love lives in God, and God in him." As the verse says, "we rely on the love God has for us" not on our love for God. There is no need to be depressed because we are dead to sin and freed from it. There is no need to be anxious as God is working all things together for my good and yours. You also say that you are striving for perfection. But let me tell you some good news. You cannot get any better, improve yourself. It has been done. The first step was to crucify you with Christ. All the stuff you are doing is to try to shape up a dead man. There is nothing that you can do to get any better. But the good news is you don't have to. When we know and believe who we are in Christ and that He is our life and we are dead to sin is when we begin to live free. The truth is that we have been made perfect. Because by one sacrifice he has made perfect forever those who are being made holy (Heb. 10:14). If we are complete in Christ ("In Him you have been made complete" - Col. 2:10) and He is our life, how could we be any less. The key is Gal. 2:20, "I have been crucified with Christ and I no longer live, but Christ lives in me. The life I live in the body, I live by faith in the Son of God, who loved me and gave himself for me". The verse is not telling you to do anything but believe the truth that sets you free. You keep saying all the things that you are doing and have done, BUT there is nothing to do. "Oh, foolish Galatians! Who has cast an evil spell on you? For the meaning of Jesus Christ's death was made as clear to you as if you had seen a picture of his death on the cross. Let me ask you this one question: Did you receive the Holy Spirit by obeying the law of Moses? Of course not! You received the Spirit because you believed the message you heard about Christ. How foolish can you be? After starting your new lives in the Spirit, why are you now trying to become perfect by your own human effort? Have you experienced so much for nothing? Surely it was not in vain, was it? I ask you again, does God give you the Holy Spirit and work miracles among you because you obey the law? Of course not! It is because you believe the message you heard about Christ." Gal. 3:1-5).

78

I have been a Christian for nearly a decade and am battling some addictive problems. I have done everything I know to get free and am not sure how to. I have talked with some Christian leaders and they either have just given me pet answers and sent me on my way, or didn't seem to know what to do. I have been trying to resist not giving up, because I am afraid that if I reach out more, then I will just keep running into the same walls. I am starting to get desperate, because I truly love God and want to serve Him and pursue holiness, but I am really battle weary. Please feel free to contact me on my phone, or by email when you have some free time. Thank you.

You are actually in a very good place to find your freedom and experience it. Until we reach the point that we are convinced beyond a shadow of a doubt that apart from Christ we can do nothing (John 15:5), there is no hope for freedom from addiction. I know it doesn't feel like it, but the "truth that sets you free" is that as a new creation in Christ, you are dead to sin and freed from it and you have been crucified with Christ. "It is no longer I who live, but Christ who lives in me. And the life I now live in the flesh I live by faith in the Son of God, who loved me and gave himself for me." (Gal. 2:20). That is the truth I learned 32 years ago that set me free from addiction. You don't feel like it and it takes revelation to know and believe it, but "desperation is the key to revelation". No one really gets free until they come to the end of self. Desperation occurs when we come to the end of self and know that we can do NOTHING to get free or live the Christian life. Paul put it like this "Indeed, in our hearts we felt the sentence of death. But this happened that we might not rely on ourselves but on God, who raises the dead." (2 Cor. 1:9). Send me your mailing address and I will send you a few resources. Also check out our website, which has quite a few. Call me on my cell phone if you want to talk.

What About the 12 Steps? What's not covered in the 12 steps that is essential to freedom? What's Wrong with The 12 Steps?

What About the 12 Steps? What's not covered in the 12 steps that is essential to freedom? What's Wrong with The 12 Steps?
Absolutely Nothing! Everything they cover is helpful and good. The problem is what they don't cover. They don't cover what is necessary for a person to be free. This is a list of what's not covered.

1. The Person of Christ—Christ is our life
2. The Work of Christ—God's only answer is in the cross
3. Forgiveness—God's only answer for anger
4. Our identity in Christ—When we know who we are in Christ is when we get free
5. Grace—God's method of dealing with us
6. Faith—The only way we receive anything and everything that God has for us
7. God's unconditional love and acceptance—All who are addicted don't know
8. The part and work of the Holy Spirit—to illumine us and give us wisdom
9. An answer for guilt and condemnation—All who are

addicted are under condemnation
10. Our position in Christ gives us victory over Satan
11. Spiritual warfare—How to win the battle
12. Our co-crucifixion frees us from power of sin
13. Dying to the law frees us from performing
14. Dying to the world frees us from demands of others
15. The part of the flesh (our learned independence)
16. Prayer
17. The Word of God

Ok, I will ask my team about the devotional. We all have the Helping Others Overcome Addiction Book. And most of us have read it. What resources do you recommend to conduct the recovery class?

I assume the recovery class is for those who are involved in the recovery ministry. If so, I would suggest going through the "Helping Others Overcome Addictions" book. It is the latest and most updated and the first seven chapters cover the problem of addiction and God's Answer for addiction. The second part of the book is about helping others and how to have a ministry of grace in the church (pages 97 to 136), and how to set up a recovery ministry (pages 137-159), and there are 14 resources to use listed as well (pages 161 to 198). I do not recommend going through the Freedom From Addiction Workbook in a class; several have tried, including myself, and it just doesn't work in that environment. The reason is that it is a 200-page workbook that requires a lot of motivation, commitment and effort which very few struggling with an addiction possess. Neil Anderson and I believe it is the best resource for someone to use to get free from their addiction, but most are not willing to do what it takes. It is best used for someone like you to take one or two through at a time who are motivated to do the work it requires. Keep in touch and let me know how things are going.

8|1

I had emailed you a couple of months ago about starting a recovery ministry in our church. You recommended that we do the Freedom from Addictive Behaviors Conference DVD's. We have one more session to do. What do you recommend we do next? Are we ready to start a class? If so, what resources would you recommend we use?

I would suggest you go through the "One Day at a Time" devotional. There are 120 devotionals with 12 devotionals on each of the ten basic truths that you need to know to be free. Each devotional is usually 2 1/2 pages with a couple of questions at the end, and a place to journal. You could cover five a week and finish in 20 weeks, but that is probably too much to cover in a week. I would suggest you cover 2 to 3 devotionals a week. Amazon has the book for $17 and I sell it for $15. I will send your first order to you with no charge for shipping. I will also send you copies of my testimony and "The Key to the Victorious Christian Life" and a packet of bookmarks (Who I am in Christ). If you need to you could copy the devotionals for anyone who couldn't afford to buy the book. Have you read "Helping Others Overcome Addictions"? It has a lot of information on how to help others and conduct a recovery ministry.

8|2

I am so confused. I am stuck in addiction to prescription drugs and bingeing. I have tried to live out who I am in Christ, but I can't help feeling that a group of believers with me is needed for support. Am I to be a Lone Ranger? I have

struggled most of my life. How do I get myself to believe,
especially when I have such a bad track record? I'm not sure
I understand how I stop myself when I go to reach for more
pills. Please help me understand. I have tried everything-
Neil Anderson's book, deliverance ministry, Bible studies,
12-step meetings, hospitalization. I feel hopeless.

A group of believers who know the truth that sets free
and their identity in Christ would be very helpful. Even
if they don't know the truth that sets free, they can offer
encouragement, fellowship and support. But they cannot
believe the truth for you, and the only way anyone
experiences their freedom from addiction is when they
believe the truth that sets free in their heart. You ask, "How
do I get myself to believe"? When most people ask that
question, they are really asking "How do I get my emotions
and experiences to measure up with that truth"? The answer
to that question is that will NEVER happen. I was freed from
my addiction to alcoholism 32 years ago when I believed
the truth of Gal. 2:20 that Christ was my life (Col.3:4) and I
was dead to sin and freed from it (Rom. 6:6, 7). What did I
do? ABSOLUTELY NOTHING! I was driving in a car with
a hangover and could not do anything. Today I know and
have been free from addiction for 32 years, but my feelings
have NEVER lined up with that truth. But I know it is the
truth that my life and my ministry are built upon. How do
you get yourself to believe? I believe it will happen when
you realize that your feelings, experiences and what others
say is not the truth, but what Jesus says, and Jesus said
"Then you will know the truth, and the truth will set you
free." (John 8:32). Our feelings seldom tell us the truth, and
we have an enemy who continually lies to us. The world is
under the power and influence of Satan and our flesh (our
reason, intellect, emotions) does not tell us the truth. You
say that you are "so confused". There is only one remedy
for confusion, and that is THE TRUTH. The truth is that
you are loved, forgiven, accepted, righteous, freed from

sin and dead to it and complete in Christ who is your life, regardless of how you feel, what you have done or not done or what anyone else says. When you begin to believe that truth is when the confusion will clear up and you begin to live in the freedom that has been given to you. You say that you have tried "everything" and that is a good thing. We have to try everything that we think might work and learn that there is nothing to do to get free. It is only when we are convinced beyond a shadow of doubt that apart from Jesus we can do nothing (John 15:5) and there is nothing we can do to get free. Unfortunately, this doesn't usually happen until we have spent our last buck and shot our last bullet. In other words, when we have come to the end of self and our resources and experience brokenness. That was the best day of my life because I could then receive the revelation from God of who I was in Christ and what I had in Him. DESPERATION IS THE KEY TO REVELATION. The apostle Paul put it like this, "We do not want you to be uninformed, brothers, about the hardships we suffered in the province of Asia. We were under great pressure, far beyond our ability to endure, so that we despaired even of life. Indeed, in our hearts we felt the sentence of death. But this happened that we might not rely on ourselves but on God, who raises the dead. You have to come to the end of self before you can rely on God who raises the dead." (2 Cor. 1:8-9).

83

I know you mean well by what you are teaching, but I am clean and sober 45 years, and from that day have dedicated my life to helping others do it also. I have done a lot of street ministry working with the mentally ill, the addicts and the down and outers. I had a Christian Men's home for many years. I have never tried to make money doing it. That was a promise I made to God before I even knew if he was really there. It was A.A. that saved my life, and it was through them where I started understanding there is a higher power. It took my 23 more years before I gave my life to Christ and knew for sure there was a God. Your method of teaching may work for some. However, we do not all get the great awakening at once. For many of us it takes time. I have spent many hours detoxing guys in motel rooms. I would never, ever try drinking again. I do not believe in testing God. When I made a statement on your webinar, you blew off my opinion as if I knew nothing. We are all different people with different ways of seeing things, and different needs. You stated that you have a beer at times. Maybe you were not really an alcoholic. I was a fetal alcohol baby. My dad gave me a sip of beer when I was very young, and I remember the anger I had when he took it away. Dad died when I was 15. I drank daily from the age of 15 to 23, searching for the ultimate high, but always passed out before I got there. I understand now the ultimate high to me was death. I had 2 suicide attempts in my last year of drinking. Finally, I had to make the decision do I live or die. My detox was one of the worst experiences in my life. I have since had 22 heart surgeries/procedures over the last 32 years. I have always found that I have to try to understand each individual who wants help, before God can use me to help that person. There is no one way that will help everyone. Thank you for listening.

Thank you for sharing your heart and part of your story and journey. We all have one, don't we? I have been clean and sober for 32 years but have also been free from addiction that long. I realize we hold totally different beliefs, but I do have the utmost respect for you. Your testimony is amazing. I believe a large part of our difference is that you and I have a different focus in our ministries. You have dedicated your life to helping others get clean and sober. I have dedicated my life to helping others experience freedom in Christ. I have worked with the mentally ill, addicts and down and outers as I make myself available to anyone who wants help, but have never done street ministry. I understand where you are coming from in that it was AA that saved your life. You mention my "method of teaching" but I really don't have a method, but my goal is to present "the truth that sets free" that Jesus referred to in John 8:32. You said "we do not all get the great awakening at once". I did not get it all at once. I was 51 years old when I found my freedom and had been a Christian 18 years, had graduated from seminary, served in the pastorate and struggled with addiction to alcohol for eight years. I know many who like you believe it is tempting God to take a drink, but I am completely convinced that I am not an alcoholic or a recovering one. I totally believe that the only reason I struggled with addiction was that I believed a lie that I was a sorry sinner who was insecure, inadequate, inferior, guilty, and an addict. When I believed "I have been crucified with Christ and I no longer live, but Christ lives in me. The life I live in the body, I live by faith in the Son of God, who loved me and gave himself for me" (Gal 2:20), and that Christ was my life (Col. 3:4) and I was dead to sin and freed from it (Rom. 6:67), I was gloriously free! How could I not be if those verses are true? You said that maybe I'm not an alcoholic because I have a beer now and then. But I struggled with it for eight nightmarish years and was destroying everything in my life that was good. I went through two treatment centers, attended 100's of AA meetings, went through 5 sponsors, was called before my church's discipline committee for being a drunk and sent to a treatment center. Everyone in my life doubted I was a Christian including my wife, my two best friends, my pastor and the assistant pastor with whom I had graduated from seminary. I know that if it had not been for God's grace that today I could be dead, institutionalized, incarcerated, or worse, still in my addiction. Jesus saved my life, but more importantly He gave me His life, which is eternal, abundant and free and He lives in me AND IS MY LIFE! I believe the secret to the victorious Christian life and the key to freedom from addiction is found in Col. 1:27, "To them

God has chosen to make known among the Gentiles the glorious riches of this mystery, which is Christ in you, the hope of glory". If Christ is our life and is living His life in us, is that not the answer for you and me and every person struggling with an addiction, life-controlling problem, besetting sin, and thorn in the flesh? I am not trying to convince you or dispute with you, but simply sharing from my heart where I'm coming from. Please do not think you have to respond and do not if you had rather not. I'm writing this primarily for my benefit and felt a need to put it in writing. You said that I have always found that I have to try to understand each individual who wants help, before God can use me to help that person and I will take that to heart. Perhaps my issue is that I disagree with you when you said "There is no one way that will help everyone". I am completely convinced that a person who has received Christ and believes he has been crucified with Christ and no longer lives, but Christ lives in them and is living their life, and they live by faith (Gal. 2:20) in that truth, will be free indeed (John 8:36). Everyone I have seen who has believed that experienced their freedom at that time. I believe that is the truth for everyone on the face of the earth. Probably my issue is that I am so passionate about "the truth that sets free" I may not try to understand where they are coming from as you pointed out. I appreciate your doing so. May the Lord bless you and prosper you and your ministry. I will be praying for you.

84

Thanks for sharing your story. I had 30 years of drinking, the last 10 years as a daily drinker. I have been in AA, keeping sober, growing spiritually, reasonably happy and useful for nearly 9 years. I discovered FICM and your website recently through a Christian friend and accountability partner. You are no doubt aware that AA's position in regards to people who have genuinely been addicted to alcohol is "once an alcoholic, always an alcoholic" and that absolute abstinence is the only answer. My question after reading your site and the FICM pages: is the AA position correct, or is a "cure" through Christ and following your steps actually possible. Thanks in advance for your answer.

Sorry to have taken so long to get back to you. There is a monumental difference between sobriety and freedom. It is as different as day is to night. Sobriety depends on the person. It is up to you to follow the steps, do the right things such as go to meetings, read the big book, don't drink or drug, don't get hungry, angry, lonely, or tired and avoid certain people, places and things. It is all up to the person. And if it is up to us, it usually leads to disaster. Although the former questioner says he has been sober a very long time, there is a huge difference between sobriety and freedom. I sincerely believe that a big reason I am free today is because I couldn't accept the world's answer for addiction (12 Steps etc.) I was a student of scripture and spent a lot of time studying and memorizing it and it seemed that freedom was a large part of it, but I still didn't understand and believe the "truth" that sets free". Freedom is not up to us. There is nothing for the Christian to do, as it has already been done in the finished work of Christ (John 19:30). What do we have to do? Nothing! Freedom has already been given to us. Anyone who is in Christ is a new creation; old things have passed away and all things are new (2 Cor. 5:17). What we have "to do" is believe the truth that we are dead to sin and freed from it (Rom. 6:6, 7) and Christ is our life (Col. 3:4) and is living his life in me and through me. As I write this, I realize that not a lot of Christians are comfortable with that. But I am convinced that the most overlooked and liberating truth in the Christian life is just that, and the ones I know who believe it are the ones who are living in freedom, grace, peace, joy and fulfillment. I believed it 32 years ago, and it is the foundation and the cornerstone of

126

my ministry. Someone asked me on the webinar last night if I had changed my view on addiction since that event 32 years ago and my answer was simply NO! I think I have matured in my thinking on grace and identity but I have not changed my core belief. If you are dead to sin and freed from it (Rom. 6:6, 7) and you know sin is not your master as you are not under law, but under grace (Rom. 6:14), what else would anyone need to know? If I know that Christ is my life (Col. 3:4), what else is there? What is the key truth we need to know to walk in freedom? "I have been put to death on the cross with Christ; still I am living; no longer I, but Christ is living in me; and that life which I now am living in the flesh I am living by faith, the faith of the Son of God, who in love for me, gave himself up for me" (Gal. 2:20 BBE). Anyone who believes this is free. Of course, that is probably the hardest thing we will ever do as everything in this world testifies against it. I was a Christian for 18 years, a seminary graduate and a former pastor before I believed it. I knew the verse and had also memorized Colossians 3 and Romans 6 and would quote them during times of temptation and it never helped me. But when I believed a half of a verse that I was dead to sin (Rom 6:2) I experienced my freedom 32 years ago. I haven't lived a perfect life as my wife will testify, but I have been free from addiction since then. As to your question, "is a 'cure' through Christ and following your steps actually possible?" There are no steps to follow as your freedom and mine has been accomplished through the finished work of Christ. Our old self was crucified with Christ and we were dead, buried and raised up with Him. I know that is a difficult thing to believe, but God's revelation of His liberating power of love, grace and freedom is only received by faith. But it seems like most of us have forgotten or overlooked the fact that we live by faith, not by sight (2 Cor. 5:7). You might ask; how do we do that? I have never seen it happen until we come to the end of self and our resources. In other words, "brokenness". 2 Cor. 1:9, 10 describes that, "We do not want you to be uninformed, brothers, about the hardships we suffered in the province of Asia. We were under great pressure, far beyond our ability to endure, so that we despaired even of life. Indeed, in our hearts we felt the sentence of death. But this happened that we might not rely on ourselves but on God, who raises the dead." The reason for that is that we will not give up on ourselves until we are completely convinced that apart from Christ we can do nothing (John 15:5). As long as we think there is something that we can do (steps, principles (biblical or not), etc.), it is not going to happen. Email me your regular mailing address and I will send you a few resources.

85

Blessings and praise God for your ministry. I am a Christian but also a functioning alcoholic. It has ruined most of my life—I'm now 51 and just about rock bottom. Any attempt I have made to follow your truthful and biblical advice is usually swept away by a tidal wave of remorse and regret at what I have lost and never really had. I wonder if you have any advice for dealing with this overwhelming burden of sadness and hopelessness and regret over my past actions. The cares of each day just sweep me under and I cannot see Christ.

Let me begin by saying that you have not ruined your life. God will use every failure and sin for your good, as He tells us in Romans 8:28. I was 51 years old when I found my freedom in Christ. I had been a Christian for 18 years, was a seminary graduate, former pastor, and had been struggling with alcoholism for eight years. It took that to bring me to the end of self (rock bottom) where I was totally convinced that apart from Christ I could do nothing (John 15:5) in my resources, i.e. my strength and wisdom. Because of that 8 year struggle I now have a successful ministry, have co-authored 5 books on freedom from addiction, and have a great marriage. The apostle Paul put it perfectly in 2 Cor. 1: 8, 9 quoted in the previous answer. You say that you are close to rock bottom and that is exactly where I was and where you have to be before you will give up on self and look to God and find His answer. What does it take? Only God knows and only He can bring anyone to the end of self. But I've heard Neil Anderson say many times it was the best day of his life and I say the same thing as it was then that I could "rely not on myself, but on God who raises the dead" (2 Cor. 1:9). You say that any truthful and biblical advice is usually swept away by remorse and regret, and you cannot see Jesus. That is a bald-faced lie from Satan. Of course, you can see Jesus. He lives in you and is your life. But if you believe the lies of Satan and believe your emotions are telling you the truth, your behavior will not confirm that. That is a large part of our problem as there is no advice you can follow that will help you or me or anyone. Jesus was not giving us advice when He said, "Then you will know the truth and the truth will set you free" (John 8:32). Jesus was making a statement of fact that when you know the truth and believe you will experience the freedom that you already have. He is not telling us to do anything but believe the truth. When the disciples came to Him and asked, "What must we do to do the works God requires?" Jesus answered, "The work of God is this: to believe in the one he has sent." (John 6:28). There is nothing to do as it has already been done. Gal. 2:20 sums it up.

Here again the answer has been provided and again there is nothing for you to do but believe that Jesus died on the cross for the total forgiveness of all your sins, past, present and future. That is the basic gospel, and as Rom. 8:1 says, there is no more condemnation (shame, regret, remorse) if you are in Christ. When we believe the basic gospel of what Christ did for us and what we have as a result of that is when we live free. There is no more guilt, shame, judgment and condemnation unless the cross didn't work. The last judgment for the Christian was at the cross. When you believe that the old sinner self you were was crucified with Christ, and you no longer live but Christ is your life and is living in you, and that you are dead to sin and freed from it (Rom. 6:6, 7), that is when you begin to live in the freedom from addiction that you already have. I don't believe most Christians really believe this, and I'm certain that those struggling with an addictive behavior do not believe it. There is only one reason that Christians don't live free, and that is DECEPTION. When we know who we are in Christ and what we have in Christ, we live free from all bondage. You say that you cannot see Christ, but I wonder where you are looking? He is no longer on the cross but lives in you and is your life (1 Cor. 6:17). When you know and believe, this is when you live free. Most ask, "How do I do this?" There is not a how to do it. Most are really asking, "How do I get my emotions and experiences to line up with this truth?" and the answer is you don't and you can't. I have been freed from my addiction for 32 years and my emotions and experiences have not perfectly lined up with the truth, but praise God I have been free from addiction for 32 years.

86

I am writing for your counsel, please. I am a licensed social worker who practices biblical counseling, and I use Neil Anderson's "Steps to Freedom" in my practice. I am presently working with a 49-year-old man who has been addicted to cocaine since the age of 13. He has 4 children and has been separated often from his wife in the last 20 years that they have been married (he is the one who leaves). He was raped by a man shortly before he started using and blames this event for his addiction. The Lord supernaturally delivered him from cocaine in the month of May of this year, which is when I began to work with the family (through the school system because of the impact the marital conflict was having on the children). It soon became apparent that he was dealing with many issues that presented as rage and anxiety. He has difficulty understanding the need for accountability and discipleship and did not follow through on the tasks he agreed to work on in the course of our sessions together (individual, couple and family meetings). He believes he is born again. He had a relapse 3 weeks ago and has avoided meeting with me since then. His wife is at her wit's end and is ready to divorce him but is waiting on God for supernatural intervention because she does not want to give up on him or their marriage. I have followed your webinar and I remember how you highlighted the importance of consequences, which your wife upheld, that helped you make a decision for freedom. This is not how he and his wife have functioned in the past. He came and went as he pleased without consequences. His pastor is of the opinion that he needs deliverance and that his will is overtaken by demonic forces which makes it impossible for him to choose freedom and has asked his wife to pray and fast for him. I am of the opinion that he can even in his relapsed state choose to submit to God and seek accountability. Please advise.

There are several issues as you have pointed out in your email and until they are resolved he will not be able to receive the help he needs.
1) He blames the rape for his addiction. No doubt that it is a factor, but that does not stop him from turning to the Lord and receiving His deliverance available to him. Many people have suffered the same, and many had worse but still found their freedom. The truth is that no one receives their freedom until they have completely given up of themselves and experienced brokenness. Sometimes you just have to let people go through what they are choosing to do until they can receive help. You really can't help anyone who is not ready to receive it. I know and respect you that you would really like to help him, but we usually have to wait until they're ready to receive it and only God can bring him to

that point.

2) It seems like his wife is not willing to let him receive the consequences of his bad behavior and that is a real problem. The fact is that her enabling him is enabling him to continue in his addiction. I don't encourage divorce, but I have observed many times that separation can lead to reconciliation.

3) There is a scriptural basis for dealing with someone like him in Matt. 18:15-17, but few churches are willing to do it. I cover it in "Helping Others Overcome Addictions" Chapter 8. Do you have a copy of it? We wrote the book to give guidance to those who are seeking to help those who are addicted. The truth is that, in my observation, no one will be able to receive help until they are confronted with tough love and someone who speaks "the truth in love."

4) As long as he is not made to suffer the consequences of his behavior, there is not much help available for him. The people who allow him to do this are actually enabling him in his ungodly behavior.

5) I agree with you that he could turn to the Lord in his relapsed state, but since he does not have to suffer consequences it will be much more difficult for him to do so.

87

I'm frustrated and am feeling the negative effects of the smoking. My thought is to throw the cigs away (have done sooo may times) and trust God....although I go and buy a pack again. I do have Chantrex, patches, and gum. I feel like I'm in rebellion. Just wanted to share. I'll continue to re-listen to the videos.

My advice is "Do not throw the cigarettes away and buy a pack if you want to". All of that is just self-effort, which is not helpful. Just keep reminding yourself of the truth of who you are in Christ and that you are dead to sin and freed from it (regardless of your actions, thoughts and feelings) and trust God to show you that you are free indeed. It may take a while for the physical effects to subside, but don't worry about it. Just stop trying to quit, relax and rest in Christ and let Him do it. He is your life.

My problem now is I don't see old self crucified. Why? I experienced this crucifixion with Christ about 25 years ago. Don't know what happened to it or how to get it to operate again in my life? What is wrong?

I believe that what is wrong is that you do not feel that your old self is crucified but very much alive and kicking and resisting, and you are trying to get your feelings to measure up with the truth which will never happen! When you know and believe the "truth that sets you free" then and only then will you see your old self crucified with Christ, but it will not last. The Christian life is lived by faith, not by feelings. Our feelings can vary widely and probably will in your case and mine. Your feelings have NOTHING to do with the fact and the truth that your old self was crucified with Christ and you no longer live but Christ lives in you (Gal. 2:20). How do you do that? Do you believe God when He said it in Gal. 2:20? You can't make it truer than it already is. What do you do? NOTHING! Any and all of our efforts to make it true is a blatant act of unbelief and is calling God a liar. "What then? If some did not believe, their unbelief will not nullify the faithfulness of God, will it? May it never be! Rather, let God be found true, though every man [be found] a liar, as it is written, 'THAT YOU MAY BE JUSTIFIED IN YOUR WORDS, AND PREVAIL WHEN YOU ARE JUDGED.'" (Rom. 3:3, 4). God's word is true and you can believe it regardless of your behavior, thoughts and feelings or what anyone else says.

How can I experience my freedom and not experience Christ as my life? I want to be free indeed, the whole thing, all of it.

The short answer is that you cannot. "Freedom" and "Christ as life" are inextricably tied together. You cannot experience freedom without experiencing Christ as your life. When you receive Christ as your Savior, you receive Him into your life. He lives in you and is your life. Many Christians, however, are not experiencing Christ as their life and are not experiencing freedom. There is no freedom outside of Christ. Freedom is part of the package. When you receive Christ, you receive freedom. Experiencing that freedom is not automatic. I did not experience it for the first 18 years of my Christian life as I didn't understand and believe the truth of Gal. 2:20. You experience it as you believe the truth that you are free, "It is for freedom that Christ has set us free. Stand firm, then, and do not let yourselves be burdened again by a yoke of slavery." (Gal. 5:1). I believe most Christians are burdened by a yoke of slavery, which is the law. Anytime we decide what we are going to do to live the Christian life we put ourselves under the law, and the law is a ministry of death (2 Cor. 3:7) and condemnation (2 Cor. 3:9). There is only one Christian life, and that is Christ's life and He lives in you. There is nothing you or I can do to get closer to God as He lives in us. As I have said many times, Gal. 2:20 is the key truth that sets people free. There are many Christians who are not experiencing "Christ as life", probably most of them. Neil Anderson has said that 90% are not. But the majority of them are not addicted to drugs, alcohol or sex as you may be and I was and it does not bring on the great suffering we experienced. However, I consider it a blessing in disguise. If I had not gone through the eight years of my addiction, I do not think I would be free today as I would not have known Christ as my life and there is no doubt I would not have the marriage I do today.

I know for sure I'm going to have to set boundaries when I get out (of prison). I have a great family, a very big family, and they all live close by and have get-togethers all the time where there is drinking; nothing that's out of control, but I just know that just as I've had to set boundaries in here, I will have to do the same out there walking very wisely day by day!

I would pray about setting boundaries as that sounds an awful lot like self-effort, which is nothing but legalism. 90% of Christians depend on what they do (all good things to do) and that is the reason 90% of Christians are not experiencing their freedom in Christ. There is nothing to worry about. Christ not only has your back, but your life and every detail of it. IT IS FINISHED! Once we start depending on ourselves it is a very slippery slope into bondage. Trying to avoid sin will lead a person right back into bondage. Don't try to shape up the old person you were. That person is dead, gone, and no more. You can't shape up a dead person. Dead = Dead. Don't ask God to forgive you. You are forgiven. To ask God to forgive you is unbelief. Stop asking God to deliver you. You are delivered and set free and dead to sin. If Christ is your life, what do you need to shape up? NOTHING! You need to believe the truth and the truth will set you free (John 8:32) and "when the Son sets you free, you are totally free (John 8:36)". "Faithful is He who calls you who also will do it." (1 Thess. 5:24). When the disciples came to Jesus and asked, "What must we do to do the work of God?" Jesus answered, "This is the work of God that you believe in the One He has sent" (John 6:39).

91

Just discovered your website; seems like a great ministry. I was in bondage/addiction for many, many years (freedom only through Christ's unconditional grace, love, forgiveness, and mercy). With 60 years of wrong thinking and believing, it is a continual reprogramming process through Christ.

Just remember in your reprogramming that it is all to the "truth that sets free". And the truth is that your old self was crucified with Christ and no longer lives, but Christ lives in you and you now live by faith (Gal. 2:20), that Christ is your life (Col. 3:4) and you are dead to sin and freed from it (Rom. 6:6, 7). Sin is no longer an issue for the Christian. It has been taken care of and is no more. IT IS FINISHED!!! The truth is that you are completely and totally free (Gal., 5:1). Of course, your feelings don't measure up to that truth and that is what most Christians struggle with, but the fact is that our emotions will never completely measure up to the "truth that sets free". I believe that's why the apostle Paul said "It is for freedom that Christ has set us free. Stand firm, then, and do not let yourselves be burdened again by a yoke of slavery." (Ga. 5:1). The yoke of slavery is the law. Once we decide what we are going to do to stay free, do right and avoid sin, we are burdened again with the yoke of slavery (the law; self-effort).

92

I'm loving the content. I just stumbled upon this somehow through Facebook. I have been reading through some of your archives and some stuff is really resonating with me. Awesome stuff. The truth has been the only thing that has freed me from addiction. Learning who I am in Christ has definitely impacted my life. Thanks for the confirmation that

I was not crazy. LOL. I have opposed some drug counselors last year through a post and was basically shunned because I believe that addiction is basically a symptom of a much bigger problem like you mentioned in one of your blogs. They didn't like that idea at all. These are counselors that are putting people's lives in their hands. They sweep the statistics under the rug and deny the recidivism rates to keep their positions. I was an addict ever since I was eight years old and I'm 47 now, I've been through every program known to man and the only thing that actually freed me was learning who I am in Christ, and even still then I sometimes went back to that addiction in my immaturity. But no secular counseling or rehabilitation center worked ever on me. In fact, when my parents insurance ran out they early graduated me. Go figure.

You have found the "truth that sets free". In the 32 years since I found my freedom, I have observed that no one finds freedom until they believe the truth of who they are in Christ. NO ONE! By the way, I was 51 years old when learned who I was in Christ and that Christ was my life (Col. 3:4) and I had been crucified with Christ (Gal. 2:20) and I was dead to sin and freed from it (Rom. 6:6, 7). That was 32 years ago and after I had served in the Pastorate and had graduated from seminary. Yes, I am 83 years old and still in the ministry and loving what I am doing telling Christians who they are in Christ. The reason secular counseling and rehabilitation centers don't work is that they don't know and don't teach identity in Christ, as it is only available through the finished work of Christ and a personal relationship with Christ. However; that being said, very few Christians know who they are in Christ (probably 15% or less). Why is that? Because it is an issue of grace and most Christians and Christian treatment centers are not grace oriented, and identity is an issue of grace. It is an issue of grace because there is nothing to do as IT IS FINISHED and every Christian is free and all you have to do to be free is believe it!!! When people came from the house of Jairus the synagogue ruler and told Him, "'Your daughter is dead,' they said, 'Why bother the teacher any more?'" (Mark 5:35), Jesus said, "Don't be afraid, JUST BELIEVE"!!! (Mark 5:36).

You have said that you have a list of over 100 Christians treatment centers? Don't you recommend that Christians should go to one?

Not necessarily, but I would much rather they go to a Christian one than a secular one. My major reservation is that the large majority of them are not grace oriented and do not teach them who they are in Christ. The one I went to was Christ-centered and God used it in my life. But it was over two years later driving down the highway listening to a tape (32 years ago) that I heard and believed who I was in Christ and found my freedom. However, I am very grateful for that Christian treatment center. God used it in my life to change my attitude toward my wife and to save my marriage.

How can you say the Christian treatment you attended and others as well were Christ-centered, but you would not necessarily recommend it?

Don't get me wrong. I have referred many people to Christian ones. As I mentioned earlier, most do not teach identity in Christ and are not grace oriented and I have never seen anyone get free until they learn who they are in Christ and there is NOTHING to do but believe the truth that they are already free as a result of Christ's finished work on the cross. That is grace, and I have found that few

Christian treatment centers and few churches really teach that. This is just an observation, but I believe that very few who attend Christian treatment centers get free as a result of it. Don't get me wrong, I have a list of over a hundred Christian treatment centers and refer people to them all the time, but going to a Christian treatment will not set anyone free until they believe who they are in Christ.

Since I talked with you things have gotten worse. She's now in the hospital on a mental health hold. I don't know if they'll release her to treatment or just release her. It's such a helpless feeling. I am reading the "Helping Others Overcome Addictions" and I believe it. I just don't know if she is ready to accept her identity in Christ yet. You went to treatment a couple of times. Do you think you could have accepted your identity and the finished work on the cross earlier had you known? Or was the process you went through necessary and then also the revelation of the truth by the Holy Spirit.

I believe the process I went through was necessary. That process was brokenness in order to bring me to the end of myself and my resources. I believe that brokenness is what has to take place so that we can receive God's revelation of the truth that sets free. DESPERATION IS THE KEY TO REVELATION. Check out what the apostle Paul said about it…"we were under great pressure. Far beyond our ability to endure, so that we despaired even of life. Indeed in our hearts we felt the sentence of death. But that happened that we might not rely on ourselves, but on God who raises the dead." (2 Cor. 1:8,9).

Hi Mike....., I have spoken with you before. Your testimony resonates with me because they are so similar. I was in the insurance business for a number of years before going to seminary to get a degree in pastoral counseling. When I got my degree, I began a ministry in counseling that God really honored and I was asked to speak at many churches in our area. That continued for a number of years until I started having trouble sleeping. My doctor at the time prescribed a very high dose of Xanax, which worked wonders, but eventually made me very depressed. After tying 21 different antidepressant medications, I just decided to go back to my college years and use alcohol to help me. And it did! A very good job. But like you, it has caused me a whole host of problems with family, church, and ministry. Like you, I have tried treatment, counseling, prayer, fasting, etc., etc, etc! But here is my problem. I've read all the material you have sent me and I have read all of Neil's books, even led others through the steps to freedom with success, but I have not found that freedom!!!! It's not like I don't understand the process and believe that it is true; for some reason, it doesn't work for me!! I would like to talk to you again, if possible.

I don't want to be rude but to just get your attention I will say this, "I don't think you understand the process as there is no process". The reason there is no process is that you have already received all that Christ died to give you. The only process is you coming to the end of self as I stated in the answer above. There is no biblical process to freedom as you are already free. I know you have been through a lot and I understand completely as I struggled for eight long years of a nightmare from hell until I hit rock bottom and knew without a shadow of a doubt that apart from Christ I could do nothing (John 15:5). But in those eight years I was trying everything anyone suggested and anything anyone told me to get free. ALL TO NO AVAIL! THE HARDER I TRIED AND THE MORE I DID THE DEEPER I WENT INTO ADDICTION!!! Finally, one day after my wife had kicked me out of the house and I was driving out of town listening to Bill Gillham teach on Romans 6 and I heard the "truth that sets free" (John 8:32) and believed it, I was free. What did I do? NOTHING! I could not do anything. I was driving in a car and had a hangover. That was 32 years ago and I have not lived a perfect life, but I have been free from addiction ever since.

I have heard you say that God uses everything in our life for good, even all our sins, failures, mistakes, suffering, literally EVERYTHING. Do you really believe that and can you give me a good example of that?

Oh yes, I believe it more today than I have ever believed as I am the best example of it of anyone I know. In the eight years I struggled with alcoholism, I was convinced I would never be in ministry again. In fact, I had fallen so far and failed so badly that when I went to a Christian treatment center I begged the Director not to tell any of the other guys that I had been in the pastorate or ministry. The large evangelical church that I was a member of had called me before the "Discipline Committee" for being a drunk. Here I am over 32 years later and have had a ministry to addicts for 32 years. I have co-authored five books on freedom from addiction, and all of them are still in print. I have had the privilege and pleasure of seeing many find their freedom in Christ over the last three decades. Vernon Terrell and I are doing four webinars a year, two of them are the "Freedom from Addiction Webinar" and two of them are based on the book, "Helping Others Overcome Addictions". My marriage was failing and almost over, but we celebrated our forty-seventh anniversary this year in May. But as Neil Anderson said, the day of my brokenness was the best day of his life as it was when I found my freedom and the beginning of Freedom in Christ Ministries. It was also the best day of my life as it was also the day I experienced my freedom and the beginning of my recovery ministry.

I'm struggling a bit. My daughter came out of detox yesterday and she didn't go to residential housing. She is living at my house. I feel I've done everything wrong so far. I have an extra car that she can drive to meetings. She has to go 5 days a week from 9 to 3. She is supposed to go to 5 AA or Celebrate Recovery meetings a week. I thought I would only let her have the car for those commitments but I ended up letting her take it to Verizon to get a replacement phone for the one she 'lost'. She doesn't have access to her money, so I paid her initial payment of $170. Now I'm regretting that. She had insurance on the old phone so it didn't have to be a total new purchase of a phone. I didn't think about the fact that she won't have money to pay the next payment without me. Now my struggle is this. Should I say she can't have the car and take her to the classes myself that she has to attend during the day and meetings at night or just let her drive my extra car? If she was using alcohol now and not in treatment, I would know that she couldn't have that freedom. But, since she is in treatment, should I help her in these ways? So, I guess I don't know if Chapter 8 in "Helping Others Overcome Addictions" on what not to do only applies when the person is refusing treatment.

You bring up an excellent point and I don't have any problem with helping a person in treatment or finding treatment or helping them in their treatment as you are doing. But you need to be prayerful about the financial help and be wise and prudent in what you do. As long as she is following the treatment plan I think what you are doing is fine. However, the main thing to keep in mind is that no plan that is dependent on what the person does will not give them freedom. Freedom is only available through the finished work of Christ.

What do you mean by "the truth that sets free"?

Millions of people in this world are struggling with various addictions. Their lives are a living death, a nightmare of hell from which they are unable to awake. I know as I lived in it for eight years. And I was a seminary graduate and an ordained minister. What was the problem? An evil sin nature, character defect, lack of faith, disobedience, etc.? NO, it was the simple issue that I didn't believe the truth that Jesus said when you know it you will be free (John 8:32). Wasn't I taught it in my years of seminary study? No, not really. Why? The seminary professors overall seemed to believe that if I just knew what they considered to be the correct theology, I would have all I needed to live a free life and be able to help others by teaching them that theology. But the truth I am talking about is so simple that it is summed up in one verse in the bible, "I have been crucified with Christ and I no longer live, but Christ lives in me. The life I live in the body, I live by faith in the Son of God, who loved me and gave himself for me." (Gal. 2:20). Did that just go right over your head? For the first 18 years of my Christian life, it went over mine. It took eight years of alcoholism to get me to a point where at the end of myself and my resources God could reveal the truth to me that Christ was my life and I no longer lived, but Christ was living my life. I know it sounds incredible as I write it, but it is the truth that sets free and God's answer for addiction. Do

I have it all figured out? Absolutely not! It is not something we can figure out. I have said many times that addiction, which is bondage, doesn't respond to common sense, logic and reason. The only way we encounter truth is via the heart, when by faith we believe the truth. "Don't be afraid, only believe" (Mark 5:36).

Why is it so important for addicts/alcoholics to be completely honest about their situation?

One major reason is that Jesus is the way, the TRUTH, and the life (John 8:32). Jesus says that Satan is a liar and the father of lies, and there is no truth in him (John 8:44). "But for the cowardly and unbelieving and abominable and murderers and immoral persons and sorcerers and idolaters and all liars, their part [will be] in the lake that burns with fire and brimstone, which is the second death" (Rev. 21:8). It seems that God has no use for liars, and we cannot get right with Him or get help unless we are honest about ourselves and our situation. BUT when we do get honest with ourselves and our situation, we tap into the help from God (and there is also an incredible amount of help available from recovery ministries, Christian counselors, churches, etc.). An addict/alcoholic has learned how to manipulate people by telling them what they want to hear. They will agree with you outwardly about their situation and agree to seek the help you want them to get, but have no intention of following through. That's why that often we have to just step aside and let God work in them to bring about what has to take place to bring them to the end of self where they are in a position to receive help.

How do we learn "how" to get free?

If I told you how you would not be able to do it. Why? Because the "how" is coming to the end of self and only God can bring a person to the end of self, however, there is something NOT to do. Stop doing all that you are doing to get free, live the Christian life, doing right, stop doing wrong, not sin, etc., because all of that is just an act of unbelief that shows you don't believe that you are dead to sin and freed from it (Rom. 6: 6, 7), that Christ is your life (Col. 3:4), that you no longer live, but Christ lives in you, and the live you now live you live by faith of the son of God who loves you and gave Himself for you (Gal.2:20), that you are now one with Christ (1 Cor. 3:17), that sin no longer has dominion over you as you are not under law, but under grace (Rom. 6:14), you have died to the law (Rom. 7:4) and your life is hidden with Christ in God (Col. 3:2).

With addiction pandemic in the world and getting worse every day "are we missing something"?

Yes, I think we are and I believe it is the fact that the majority of Christians believe that God is separate from us. Even among most pastors and committed Christians the message they have is Christ is for us, with us, and will act for us. Now I don't deny that, but that is not the whole truth. The apostle Paul told us that "the mystery hidden for ages and now revealed to us is "Christ in you, the hope of glory." (Col. 1:27). That changes everything. If Christ is our life, then what we are missing is freedom in Christ and all that goes with the "victorious Christian life." I will not go into all that as I have just listed a lot of them in my previous answer. If Christ is our life and is living it, how could anyone struggle with an addictive behavior. The only answer is that we do not know or believe "the truth that sets free," which is "Christ in you, the hope of glory". I think most Christians would give verbal assent to this, but it seems to be sadly lacking in how we live life, deal with issues and problems, and respond to Him who loved us and gave Himself for us. Do we know and believe that we were crucified with Him and we no longer live, but Christ lives in us and the life we live we live by the faith of the Son of God who loved us and gave Himself for us (Gal. 2:20)? Do we know that Christ is our life (Col. 3:4) and the only life we have? Do we know that we are one Spirit with Him (1 Cor. 6:17)? But didn't Jesus pray that we would be one with Him and the Father? I believe that prayer was answered. I know that it's hard to get your mind around that. In fact, it is impossible. But we don't live by sight but by faith. As Prov. 3:5, 6 says we can't understand that or figure it out. As it reads in the Message, "Trust GOD from the bottom of your heart; don't try to figure out everything on your own." (Prov. 3:5 MSG). If you figure it out on your own, you might come up with a well-reasoned theology, but it will not do you much good. After three years of studying theology at seminary and eighteen years as a Christian, I was an alcoholic and a falling down drunk. I had to change my theology to experience my freedom in Christ. Or a better way to put it, I had to believe Gal. 2:20. When I believed that I was "dead to sin and freed from it" I was free. I didn't do a thing to get free. In fact I had a hangover the day I believe the truth that I was no longer living, but Christ was living in me, and I have never got over it. How could you get over it? It staggers the imagination. It blows your mind? You don't grasp it with your mind. As Rom. 10:6 says, "If you confess with your mouth that Jesus is Lord and believe in your heart that God raised him from the dead, you will be saved." (Rom. 10:9 ESV). We do not believe with our minds, but our hearts. That is who you are (in your heart). Heart is spirit. Stop trying to figure it out and as Jesus responded to Jairus when they told him his daughter was dead, "Ignoring what they said, Jesus told the synagogue ruler, 'Don't be afraid; just believe.'" (Mark 5:36 NIV). Ignore the facts, the circumstances, your feelings, what others say and believe Jesus (The TRUTH).

103

What if someone is really motivated but needs some help in appropriating their freedom, would you recommend working through "The Freedom from Addiction Workbook"?

Before you begin, there are some things you absolutely must know.

1. Only truth sets you free. It will not make any difference what you do, no matter how spiritual it may be. Truth sets you free and Jesus is the TRUTH and He lives in you. As Martin Luther said 500 years ago, "Nothing you do helps you spiritually. Only faith in Christ and His word and works". In fact, if you depend on what you do, you have put yourself under law and anything you do will be counterproductive. We are set free not by how we behave, but by what we believe.

2. Working through the Workbook and a $1.00 might get you a cup of coffee, but that's all it will get you. Here again it is not what you do, but the truth you believe that sets free. The purpose is not just to get through the workbook, but to "know the truth that sets free".

3. It will not be enough to look up the Bible verses and write them down. Trust God to reveal the truth that sets free to you and pray "I keep asking that the God of our Lord Jesus Christ, the glorious Father, may give me the Spirit of wisdom and revelation, so that I may know him better. I pray also that the eyes of my heart may be enlightened in order that I may know the hope to which he has called me, the riches of

his glorious inheritance in the saints, and his incomparably great power for us who believe."(Eph. 1:17–19) as the workbook suggests before you begin and before each time you begin to work in it.

4. Be honest and open with me or your mentor you are working with. If you don't understand or agree with something, bring it up. Honesty is absolutely essential to finding your freedom from addiction. Don't play games or try to impress anybody. You only deceive yourself when you do.

5. Don't do just to get it done. Do it trusting God, believing that He will show you the truth of who you are in Christ. He is living in you and the freedom and deliverance has already been provided for you. The object is not to complete the Workbook, but to discover the truth of who you are in Christ and who He is in you and the freedom that is yours. Call me if you have questions and are dead serious about working through it.

1O4

Do you recommend "interventions" and if so, could you give me a few guidelines?

Yes, I do, and here are some guidelines to conduct a biblical intervention.

The purpose of a Biblical Intervention is to confront the destructive and sinful behavior in the life of a loved one. The intervention speaks the "truth in love" to the person. The truth brings the issue into the light where God is able to work. As long as the problem stays hidden, there will be no resolution. The truth is spoken in love and lets the person know that he is loved and that there is help available and gives them a choice to get help.

Everyone involved in the intervention must be a significant person in his or her life. If they are married, a spouse is essential in almost every case. The exception would be if the spouse is also struggling with an addictive behavior and would be unable to speak to them credibly or if they refuse to be a part of it. Others could be close relatives, such as parents, children, or anyone who knows them and is familiar with the problem. Friends, bosses, neighbors, coworkers and the pastor are all possibilities. Many are reluctant to let children participate, but they can be the most influential and persuasive. They might be too young, but in all cases the children are severely affected and understand what is going on a lot more than you would think. I led an intervention with a lady whose husband, pastor, best friend, two neighbors and a teenage daughter were involved. All of us shared with her and she was unmoved and very resistant until her teenage daughter shared with her. That did it; she broke down and agreed to do what we suggested. Her daughter went upstairs with her, helped her pack, and she checked into a treatment center that afternoon.

Speak the truth in love. Stress the fact that you love and care for them and only want the best for them. Don't tell them how sorry they are. Don't say you are sick and tired of them and are not going to put up with it anymore. The point is to help them not to give you some relief. Do not accuse them and belittle their character. The main thing you want to do is to share facts and events that have happened that demonstrate the severity of the problem. Remember, the problem is not them, but the lies they believe. Do point out their good points and how much they are loved, valued and needed. Do tell them who they are in Christ. Do encourage them that it is not too late, and that God wants to set them free and bless them, as they are a dearly loved child of His. Do let them know that when they deal with their problem, they will be welcomed back with open arms.

Before you meet, everyone that is to be involved should write out the points they are going to make. Don't wing it, you are too emotionally tied to them to do that and it will derail the whole process. Give facts of specific events that

149

have happened that were a result of their addiction—they had a hangover and didn't go to work; I had to lie to your boss; you forgot to pick the children up; you were driving drunk; you didn't come home until…; our finances have been decimated; you cussed out the neighbor, etc., whatever is factual. Tell them how it made you feel and how it affected you, the situation and others you know about. It is OK to be emotional, but stick to the facts. This makes the point much better than attacking their character. Each one should take their turn and share their prepared points they want to make. It doesn't have to be word-for-word, but you want to make your points of why they need help and not tear them down.

Expect resistance. Do not argue with them. Stay with the facts and your prepared points. When everyone is finished sharing, someone, probably the leader or someone in authority such as the pastor or their boss can share with them what they want them to do—usually go to a treatment center and to do so that day. This is important because if they don't do it then they will come up with a reason not to if it is delayed. Of course preparations will have to be made with the treatment center they will be attending. If you would like a referral to a Christian treatment Center contact MikeQ@gracewalk.org. What if they are unwilling to go to a Christian treatment center and are willing to go to a secular treatment center? We never recommend secular treatment centers, but if that's the only thing they will do then that can be part of the process and we would advise you to let them do that. Keep in mind though that secular treatment centers are very expensive and if you don't have insurance, the cost can be prohibitive.

There must be an ultimatum. Intervention will not work without one. You can do all the above, and most likely it will be totally useless without an ultimatum. I would not be involved in one without an ultimatum. If you do give an ultimatum and do not follow through, it will be just another round of venting your dissatisfaction with them and empty threats to which they will pay no attention. It would be better not to have an intervention than to have one without an ultimatum. All it will do is reinforce their belief that they can continue with their sinful and destructive behavior and you are going to do nothing about it. What should the ultimatum be? That is up to you, but it must have teeth in it. It must be tough love. Usually it is the spouse leaving or them being kicked out of the house. If their boss is involved, the loss of a job can be very persuasive. It should probably be something like that, along with the promise that none of you involved will continue with your enabling behavior and they can consider themselves cut off from anything that will enable them to continue in it. But this in itself is not enough. For an intervention to be successful, there must be an ultimatum that goes into effect immediately that will cost them something. Usually it is separation from their loved ones and their home. Remember, this is not to punish them. It is to help them. And if you are ever going to help them, you have to exercise the tough love of an ultimatum. Count the cost. They may not respond as you desire. In fact, their response may be the exact opposite of what you desire. Are you willing to accept their anger and animosity toward you, knowing that what you did was in love and to help them? Are you willing to continue living as you have been and accept their sinful and destructive behavior? The sad fact is that most are willing to do this rather than intervene and issue an ultimatum. If you are doing it just to get them to do something, don't do it! Unless you can do it in faith, trusting God with the consequences regardless, because it's the right thing to do, don't do it! However, if you do and they do have a very negative response, all is not lost. You have acted in faith, trusting God. God can use it however He wants to, and it can be part of the process. We don't know what it takes to bring a person to the end of self and their resources, but God does. You can choose to be part of the process by a decision to follow through and to stop your behavior that enables them to live outside God's will. As hard as this may be, it will be the best thing you can do for them. It will be the most loving, redemptive thing that you can do for them. In doing so you have put them in God's hands and He alone can set them free from their addictive behavior.

Remember that it is not up to you to straighten them out and fix them. Only God can bring them to the point that they will turn to Him and receive the freedom that has always been there for them. Only He knows what it is going to take to do that. You and I don't. He loves them, a lot more than you do and you can trust Him regardless of what the person does and how bad it looks. It may very well be that it might have to get a lot worse to bring the person to this point. Those of us who have finally gotten to that point wouldn't trade it for anything. Your only response is to trust God and act in faith. Yes, it will take a miracle for a person to stop their addictive behavior and experience freedom in Christ, but our God is a miracle-working God, and He has already worked the miracle necessary for this to take place. It happened on the cross over 2,000 years ago when Jesus was crucified, died, buried and resurrected and we were in Him when it happened. Many who seemed totally hopeless and beyond help are now experiencing the reality of this miracle every day. If you are in Christ you are a living, walking, breathing miracle. You are in Christ; He is in you and is your very life. If your loved one in bondage is in Christ, he is a miracle also and there is great hope for him. If not, you can pray that he would encounter Jesus, the One who gave His life for him and forgave all his sins. Don't pray for them to change their behavior. Pray that they will encounter the miracle working God who will set them free from sin, the world, the law, the flesh and the devil. "Look to Him who is able to do immeasurably more than all we ask or imagine, according to his power that is at work within us." (Eph. 3:20).

1O5

What about repentance? Isn't that essential to finding freedom?

Most Christians do not know or understand repentance. Repentance comes from the Greek word in the New testament "metanoia", which is from meta (change) and nous (mind). Most think it means to change behavior, which is part of the legalistic mindset or theology that most Christians have bought into; that it is up to them to do something (change their behavior). It would seem that they do not believe what Jesus said... "apart from Me you can do nothing" (John 15:5). And no one will experience their freedom until they believe that truth. In other words, they will not until they experience brokenness. Brokenness is coming to the end of self and knowing there is nothing to do to experience freedom because they already have it as it was purchased for them at the cross through the finished work of Christ. Jesus meant it when He said "IT IS FINISHED" (John 19:30). I believe that is probably Satan's greatest weapon and the most paralyzing lie that he has gotten most Christians to believe that they need to do something rather than BELIEVE the truth of what has already been done. Yes, it is when we repent and believe the truth of who we are in Christ that we will find our freedom. When Jesus started His ministry His message was repent and believe the gospel. "The time is fulfilled, and the kingdom of God is at hand; repent and believe in the gospel." (Mark 1:15). A major part of the Gospel is that when we repent and believe the Gospel, we receive Christ. "But as many as received Him, to them He gave the right to become children of God, [even] to those who believe in His name," (John 1:12). If we received Christ, then He is in us. I have been telling this truth to Christians for over 30 years and it seems no more than 10% of them believe it. Why?!?! You would think it is the greatest truth in the universe and it is. When a person believes this, they experience their freedom in Christ. Why don't they believe it? Because to believe this truth they must have come to the end of self (self-effort) and most of us never get there. Why?! Because we believe there is something we can do. We have not given up on ourselves. Hannah Whitall Smith sums it up: "Rather than admit helplessness, men will undergo many painful sacrifices, if only self may share the glory. A religion of bondage always exalts self. It is what I do, my efforts, my fasting, my sacrifices, my prayers. But a religion of freedom leaves nothing for self to glory in. It is all Christ and what He does." But some say, "Wait a minute, we're Americans, we never give up! We're self-starters, we're go-getters, we're hard chargers, we're high achievers. We can make it happen. We can get it done. When the going gets tough the tough get going". Fine, but that's not the Christian life. What is the Christian life? "My grace is sufficient for you, for my power is made perfect in weakness. Therefore I will boast all the more gladly about my weaknesses, so that Christ's power may rest on me. That is why, for Christ's sake, I delight in weaknesses, in insults, in hardships, in persecutions, in difficulties. For when I am weak, then I am strong" (2 Cor. 12:9, 10). Does anyone want to sign up for that? NO! Because that is the theology that sets people free, but it only sets free those who are willing to renounce self-effort and agree with Jesus that apart from Him they can do nothing. And that only comes through brokenness, but as Neil Anderson says "It was the best day of my life" and it was the best day of my life as it was then and only then that I found my freedom. What do you have to do? Believe the truth that you are dead to sin and freed from it (Rom. 6:6. 7), and Christ is your life (Col. 3:4) and is living it (Gal. 2:20).

Is there a "key" to being free and living in victory? Could

you give me a list of all the verses you use about freedom?

The key to being free and living in victory.

The key is to know and believe that God has already given everything to you. God has done it all and there is absolutely nothing for you to get or to do, but believe it, thank Him for it and live in the knowledge of that truth by faith. See below what has God already done for us. Note verbs are past tense. This is a done deal. God has done it. There is nothing left for Him to do or give you.

- Our sins have been forgiven (1 John 2:12).
- We are justified freely by His grace (Rom. 3:24)
- We were reconciled to Him by the death of His Son (Rom. 5:10)
- We died to sin and were baptized into Christ and His death (Rom. 6:2, 3).
- We have been united with Him in His resurrection (Rom. 6:5).
- Our old self was crucified with Him and we have been freed from sin (Rom. 6:6, 7).
- We died to the law and have been released from the law (Rom. 7:4, 6).
- The law of the Spirit of life set us free from the law of sin and death (Rom. 8:2).
- We received a Spirit of Sonship (Rom. 8:15).
- Christ has accepted us (Rom. 15:7).
- We were washed, sanctified, and justified in the name of the Lord Jesus (1 Cor. 6:11).
- He anointed us, set His seal of ownership on us and put His Spirit in us (2 Cor. 2:22).
- Jesus has overcome the world (John 16:33).
- We have been crucified with Christ and Christ lives in us (Gal. 2:20)
- Through the cross, the world has been crucified to us and us to the world (Gal. 6:14).

- We have been made complete in Christ (Col. 2:10).
- We died with Christ to the basic principles of the world (Col. 2:20).
- Jesus canceled the written code (law) that was against us (Col. 2:14).
- Jesus disarmed the powers and authorities (Satan and his demons) (Col. 2:15).
- We died with Christ, and our lives are now hidden with Christ in God (Col. 3:3).
- God raised us up with Christ and seated us with Him in the heavenly realm (Eph. 2:6)
- It is for freedom that Christ set us free (Gal. 5:1).
- God has blessed us with every spiritual blessing in the heavenly realm (Eph. 1:3).
- God has lavished the riches of His grace on us (Eph. 1:8).
- His divine power has given us everything we need for life and godliness through our knowledge of him who called us by his own glory and goodness. Through these he has given us his very great and precious promises, so that through them you may participate in the divine nature and escape the corruption in the world caused by evil desires. (2 Pet. 1:3, 4).

These verses point out we live in freedom and victory by believing the promises (His Word to us) that He has given us everything we need for life and godliness. As we believe the truth, we participate in the divine nature and escape the corruption in the world caused by evil desires. We have just scratched the surface of what God has already done for us. We will spend the rest of eternity learning and understanding it. We only need to believe the facts of what God has done for us. As you choose to believe the truth of what He has done for you; what He has given you and who you are in Christ—your behavior will change and you will live in the freedom and victory He has already provided for you! "This is the victory that has overcome the world, even our faith." (1 John. 5:4).

107

You have quoted Madame Guyon who said, "Everything is Jesus. Everything else is a lie." What does that mean?

All that is going on in this world, the worries in my life, is as Shakespeare said, "Much ado about nothing". It is essentially a "tempest in a teapot". The scenes change, the characters are different and the props are moved in and out, but they are just props. The plot however does not change. It is all about Jesus. Everything points to Jesus. Everything else is a lie. All else is a lie. All else is a sham. All reality and truth are in Jesus. Jesus + nothing = Everything. The father of lies jerks most of us around like puppets on a string. We dance to his tune when we look for life in what the world offers. It is a dance of death. But Jesus died not only for our sins. He died to sin and to this world, and so have we as we were in Him when He died, was buried, and rose from the dead. The strings have been cut and we are no longer puppets. We are in Christ and He is our life. Everything apart from Christ is death, but life lives in us. We know Him, whom to know is eternal life (John 17:3). Why do I believe that the world has anything to offer, but emptiness, ashes and death? Don't I know that I am united with Him who is eternal life? All God would have me to do is "believe in the One He has sent" (John 6:29). He came that I might have life and have it abundantly (John 10:10). But it seems like a lot of the time I shuffle around in my grave clothes. I have been raised from the dead, but the illusions and delusions that life can be found apart from Christ lead us to dead ends of despair and death. There is a faint whisper of truth within me that only in Him is life, peace, joy, freedom and fulfillment. But my feelings, the world and its values and its ruler are shouting the opposite to me. Most are building their lives, houses and careers on shifting sands. They have erected magnificent props on a stage that can be removed overnight. When God brings the curtain down on this comedy of errors, then this world we love and cherish and all the vain things that charm us most will be destroyed. Everything but Jesus will be turned to ashes. Jesus will remain, as He is eternal. So, will I as I am in Him and He is in me (John 14:20). I am eternally one with the Eternal One. I am immortal, indestructible and bulletproof. We are God's children and what we will be like has not been revealed, but we know that when He appears, we will be like Him (1 John 3:2). But the world totters, Satan rages, and my feelings run wild. I don't feel safe, it doesn't look like victory and I am sinking. Like Peter, I have taken my eyes off Jesus and am looking at the waves of oppression and deception that threaten to overwhelm me (Matt. 14:28-31). Where is the way out? What is truth? Where can I find life? Jesus says I am the way, the truth and the life (John 14:6). It is nowhere else to be found. Why do I look for, strive for, struggle for and seek what I already have? I have it all. I have Jesus. I have everything. I am complete in Christ (Col 2:10). I know that it sure doesn't feel like it, seem like it or look like it, but so what? All the opposing forces raised up against me are simply shadows in this valley of death I am walking through. There is no substance or reality to them. Victory has been won. It is all over. It is done. It is finished! Satan is defeated (Col. 2:15). Sin and everything against me has been nailed to the cross (Col. 2:14). The world has been crucified to me and I am dead to it (Gal. 6:1). What a wretched man I am! Who will rescue me from this body of death? Thanks be to God — through Jesus Christ our Lord! (Rom. 7:24, 25). I don't feel victorious and if I do, it doesn't last long. But given the choice, I would rather be victorious than have fleeting feelings that I am victorious. Christ is VICTOR! Death is swallowed up in victory (1 Cor. 15:54). What chance did it have against LIFE? But remnants of death beckon to us from this dying world. They promise, posture and pose as success, prosperity and status, but end up as ashes in our hands.

Only Jesus gives life. Jesus is Life. Jesus is all. Jesus is everything. Everything else is a lie. Jesus lives in me and I am in Him and He is my life. I am united to Him and one with Him. Is that enough? Nothing matters but Jesus and our relationship with Him. There is no life, peace, joy, freedom and fulfillment but in Him. It is really all too simple. Jesus says, "Don't be afraid, just believe" (Mark 5:36).

"I know now, Lord, why you utter no answer. You are yourself the answer. Before your face questions die away. What other answer would suffice?"
—C.S. Lewis

If you have additional questions or need more information, please contact Mike at:

4590 Mountain Creek Drive
Roswell, GA 30075
(404) 275-5122

https://FreedFromAddiction.org

FreedFrom@bellsouth.net

1O8

Appendix: The Strange Odyssey of a Legalistic Preacher Who Became a Drunk, Discovered Grace and Was Set Free. Mike Quarles' Testimony of Freedom from Addiction

When I became a Christian in 1970 at the age of 33, I was really excited. This was what I had been looking for all my life. At last I had peace and a purpose in my life. I hit the ground running. I went to church every time the doors opened. As Bill Gillham says, "If you had tied the average Baptist to me I would have dragged him to death." I wanted my life to count for God. I pursued preparation for ministry with determination and zeal.

I was the founder and President of a local Stock Brokerage firm, but I gave that up and headed off to seminary. How could I not take the message of eternal life to a lost and dying world? I graduated from seminary and went into the pastorate. It was my custom to spend at least an hour a day in Bible study and prayer. I memorized chapters of Scripture. I fasted and prayed. I read hundreds of books and listened to numerous tapes. I went to every conference that came to town. I went to Bill Gothard's conferences so many times that I lost count, including the Pastor's and Advanced ones. I witnessed to anything that moved. It was my duty -- how could I do less? My children didn't like to ride in the car with me because I would pick up hitchhikers so I could witness to a captive audience. My wife didn't like to go out in public with me because I would witness to strangers while we were waiting for our ice cream cones in Baskin-Robbins.

I tried to do everything I had been taught in order to live a successful Christian life. What was the result of all this? My wife and children didn't respect me because in my zeal to make them be good Christians, I was legalistic, harsh and unloving. My marriage was a mess and my personal life was a shambles. I came to the realization that everything I had learned about living the Christian life just wasn't working for me.

Finally I came to grips with reality and left the pastorate and went back to being a stockbroker. I became the manager of the E. F. Hutton office in Birmingham, Alabama and soon was making more money than I had ever made in my life. But I felt like such a failure. I felt I had failed God, my wife and children, and my church. I turned back to my old ways of dealing with my problems and began to drink. In a short period of time I became a full-fledged alcoholic. I didn't want to be one and tried everything I knew to stop, but nothing seemed to help. Here are some things I tried:

1. Consistent Quiet Time
2. Bible Study
3. Fasting
4. Visitation Evangelism
5. Christian Twelve Step Program
6. Accountability group
7. Hundreds of AA meetings and 5 Sponsors
8. Christian Counselors
9. Christian Psychiatrist
10. Secular Psychiatrist
11. Christian Psychologist
12. Secular Psychologist
13. Addictions Counselor
14. 3 days with an Addictions Specialist
15. Secular Treatment Center
16. Christian Treatment Center
17. Read all books on addiction I Could Find
18. Healing Of Memories Session
19. Baptism of the Spirit Session
20. Casting Out Of Demons Session (Twice)

21. Public Confession
22. Group Therapy
23. Took the Drug Antabuse
24. Disciplined By my Church
25. Rigid Schedule with Every Minute Planned
26. Many Hours Studying Scriptural Principles
27. Memorized Chapters of Scripture
28. Discipleship Groups
29. Prayer
30. Promises to God and my Wife

Why didn't any of this work? None of these were bad or wrong things to do, but all were things I was doing in the flesh and "sinful passions are aroused by the flesh" (Rom. 7:5). Whenever we commit ourselves to a program, rules, method, steps, principles, etc. to perform, we are depending on what we do and put ourselves under law and the law is what gives sin power in our lives (1 Cor. 15:56). Paul didn't say, what will set me free, but "WHO will set me free?" (Rom. 7:24). There is no "What" (program, treatment, steps, plan, method, principles, etc.) or anything you can do that can set you free, but "if the Son sets you free you are free indeed" (John 8:36).

Where did all of this get me? I was totally out of control. I was depressed for days on end and suicidal. I was like the Prodigal Son -- all I wanted was out of the pig pen. I had given up on being a good Christian and the idea of ministry seemed like a cruel joke. Jerry Clower, the Mississippi comedian tells a story that illustrates my predicament: Jerry and his buddy Marcel were out coon hunting one night and treed a big coon. Marcel climbed up the tree to shake the coon out, but when he got up there he found out it was a lynx, not a coon, and it gets after Marcel and is about to tear him up. Marcel hollers down at Jerry, "Shoot, shoot, this thang is killin me." Jerry hollers back, "I'm afraid to shoot, I might hit you". Marcel hollers back down, "Shoot up here amongst us, one of us has got to have some relief." That describes exactly where I was.

Now that was a very painful place to be but exactly where God wanted me. I learned that God's purpose for us is to bring us to the end of ourselves and our resources so that we can begin to trust Christ to be our resource and our life and to really live by faith. 2 Cor. 1:8,9 sums it up, "We were under great pressure, far beyond our ability to endure, we despaired of life. Indeed the sentence of death was in our heart. But that happened that we might rely not on ourselves, but on God who raises the dead."

Someone has said that it is when we have shot our last bullet and spent our last buck that God is able to work in our lives. There is no possibility of freedom, peace, victory and joy without coming to the end of self. The way up in the Christian life is down; revival is not the roof blowing off, but the floor caving in. Grace always flows downhill and meets us at our point of need -- at our point of failure and brokenness. Grace cannot be merited or manipulated. It is only available for those who have experienced total, absolute bankruptcy of their own self and failure of their resources.

Does God have an answer for addiction? Is there really any hope for the person who seems to be hopelessly enslaved? Is there such a thing as the victorious Christian life? I lived in constant defeat. My struggles seemed to be more intense and my defeats seemed to be more disastrous than most. But I really didn't know many, if any, Christians who seemed to be free and living the victorious Christian life. No one had any answers for me.

Now I see that not only did I not know what the answer was, but also I didn't have a clue as to what the problem was. Dr. Bill Gillham, in his book Lifetime Guarantee, puts it like this, "The problem is you don't know what your problem is. You think your problem is your main problem, but that's not the problem at all. Your problem is not your problem and that's your main problem."

What is the problem? The problem is not the bad behavior but the belief behind the behavior that causes us to act that way. Our behavior will always be consistent with our beliefs. What that means to the addict or anyone in bondage is that their problem is not drinking alcohol or doing drugs or whatever, but it is the belief (misbeliefs or lies) that causes them to act the way they do.

I teach from time to time in Christian treatment centers. I make it a point to say every time, "If you have a life-controlling problem, an addiction, etc. and want to be free, do NOT focus on the addictive behavior, but look at the beliefs that cause you to continue in the addictive and self-destructive behavior." As I reflect on my struggle to be free, it is amazing to me that I didn't question my beliefs and my theology. I did try a lot of different things, but I stubbornly held on to some established beliefs that kept me from being free. Why did I do this? Because I believed I knew the "truth" and I was convinced that my problem was not my beliefs, but my inability to put them into action. That was a lie.

As far as I knew I had tried everything there was to try. Everyone had given up on me. My pastor later told me, "I didn't know anything else to tell you." Finally a friend handed me some tapes and said, "Here, listen to these, maybe they'll help you". I had listened to a couple of these tapes before and thought, "I don't want to listen to these, this theology doesn't agree with mine" (see what I mean about stubbornly holding onto old beliefs?).

Then another thought came into my mind and I know now God was speaking to me, "Your theology is not doing you much good!!!" There was no denying the truth of that, so I made what would be one of the best decisions I would ever make -- I would listen to the tapes with an open mind. However, I went out and got drunk again. The next morning Julia strongly suggested that I go visit some friends out-of-town and give her a break. I packed a few clothes and headed to Lookout Mountain. I was driving along listening to the third tape of the Victorious Christian Life set which was "Co-crucifixion is Past Tense". Bill Gillham was teaching on our death with Christ. Rom. 6:6,7 says, "For we know that our old self was crucified with Him so that the body of sin might be done away with, that we should no longer be slaves to sin -- because anyone who has died has been freed from sin." What is this? I have died with Christ and I have been freed from sin? That's what I need, but how do I make that true in my life? Then Gillham was saying, "It is not something you do, it is something that has been done; our death with Christ is past tense, the old person that we were 'was crucified' and 'anyone who has died has been freed from sin'." And then he said, "You 'died to sin' (Rom 6:2), you are 'dead to sin' (Rom. 6:11). I know you don't act dead to sin, you don't feel dead to sin, you don't even look dead to sin, you think that is just a positional truth, that's just the way God sees me, that's just what God says about me. Listen, what God sees is reality. What God says is the truth".

It was at that moment that the lights came on and in that moment I knew the truth. I knew I had died with Christ and the old sin-loving sinner had died and was no more. Oh I had believed the lie and acted like it for all these years, but that was not who I was. I now knew the truth was that I was dead to sin whether I acted like it, felt like it, looked like it or anyone else believed it -- because God said I was. I also knew the truth that I was free, "because anyone who had died has been freed from sin" (Rom. 6:7). Jesus said, "Then you will know the truth and the truth will set you free" (John 8:32). I had believed the lie that I was a hopeless,

166

helpless alcoholic and had lived in bondage all the years that I believed it. But less than 24 hours away from a drunk, I knew without a shadow of a doubt, that I, Mike Quarles, was a child of God who was "in Christ", because I had died with Christ, was dead to sin and had been freed from sin. Free at last, free at last! Praise God I was free at last!!!!!

Rejoicing in my discovery of this truth and my freedom, I ran in to my friends house shouting that I was free. I called Julia and tried to explain to her what had happened. She thought I was on another wild goose chase and wouldn't even hear me out. It didn't dampen my enthusiasm though, as I knew who I was in Christ and that I was free. I have never doubted it since that day.

You may ask, how could anyone who had been in bondage for years and was drunk the day before be set free by listening to a tape? Actually listening to a tape did not set me free, but believing the truth that was taught on the tape did set me free. The truth is that I was free and had been ever since I became a Christian, but I had believed a lie about who I was that effectively kept me in bondage.

Neil Anderson asks in his conferences, "How many died with Christ?" Most, if not all, raise their hands. Then he asks, "How many are free from sin?" Then he says, "It better be the same hands because it clearly states in Romans 6:7, 'Anyone who has died has been freed from sin'." All Christians died with Christ so all Christians have been freed from sin. Now if they don't believe they have been freed from sin, they will probably not act like it. We always act according to our beliefs, according to how we perceive ourselves. That is why the issue is always identity. If you don't know the truth about who you are "in Christ", it doesn't make any difference how much scripture you know and how many discipleship programs you are in or how much you pray or how long your quiet time is or how accountable you are.

A big part of our problem is that we evangelicals do what we accuse the liberals of doing. We base our beliefs on our emotions and experiences. How many of us could say we "feel dead to sin"? Anyone? How many of us could say that based on our experiences we know that we are "dead to sin"? None of us, of course. So we don't believe the truth that we are "dead to sin and alive to God" and as a result we don't live in freedom and victory.

Harry Houdini, the famed escape artist from a few years back, issued a challenge wherever he went. He could be locked in any jail cell in the country, he claimed, and set himself free. Always he kept his promise, but one time something went wrong. Houdini entered the jail in his street clothes; the heavy metal doors clanged shut behind him. He took from his belt a concealed piece of metal, strong and flexible. He set to work immediately, but something seemed to be unusual about this lock. For thirty minutes he worked and got nowhere. An hour passed, and still he had not opened the door. By now he was bathed in sweat and panting in exasperation, but he still could not pick the lock. Finally after laboring for two hours, Harry Houdini collapsed in frustration and failure against the door he could not unlock. But when he fell against the door, it swung open! It had never been locked at all! But in his mind it was locked and that was all it took to keep him from opening the door and walking out of the jail cell. (Spiritual Strongholds, Don McMinn, NCM Press, Oklahoma City OK, 1993).

Christian, the door to freedom is not locked -- it was opened wide when Christ died on the cross and you died with Him. Not only have you been crucified, dead and buried, but the new creation that you are was raised up with Him (Eph. 2:6). What does it take to walk through that wide open door to freedom? All it takes is for you to believe the truth. "It was

168

for freedom that Christ set you free..." (Gal. 5:1). But if you believe that you have to struggle, strive and strain then God will allow you to do that until you collapse in frustration and failure like Houdini. That is exactly what happened to me.

I am convinced that no one will ever be free until they understand grace. For sin shall not be your master, because you are not under law, but under grace. (Rom. 6:14). In all of the people that tried to help me, no one ever said, "The problem is not you, but the lies you believe." No one ever said, "The answer is not what you do, but what Christ did on the cross." That would have really been good news. But they would say, "do this, don't do that, abstain from that, refrain from this,, etc.

Watchman Nee puts it like this in The Normal Christian Life, " It is a great thing to see that we are in Christ! Think of the bewilderment of trying to get into a room in which you already are! Think of the absurdity of asking to be put in! If we recognize the fact that we are in, we make no effort to enter."

Finally, what did I do to gain my freedom? Remember that the day before I found my freedom I had been drunk. I was driving along with a hangover listening to a tape. The answer is that I did nothing. I simply believed God. I believed that I had "died to sin" (Rom 6:2) and "anyone who has died has been freed from sin (Rom. 6:7). Notice that all these verbs are in the past tense. It has been done. IT IS FINISHED (John 19:30).

What I am saying is that these things had been true of me ever since the first day I became a Christian.
Of course they are true of every Christian, but it has absolutely no effect if they do not believe it. We always act according to what we believe. Truth sets you free (John 8:32)

and lies keep you in bondage. We do need a revelation of the truth and "Desperation is the Key to Revelation" which comes at the end of self and our resources.

During World War II, Lieutenant General Jonathan Mayhew Wainwright was commander of the Allied Forces in the Philippines. He was forced to surrender to the Japanese on May 6, 1942. For three years he suffered as a prisoner of war in a Manchurian camp. During his internment, he endured the incessant cruelties of malnutrition, physical and verbal abuse, and psychological mind-games. Through it all he maintained his dignity as a human being and soldier. But after the Japanese surrendered the war, his captors kept Wainwright and the other prisoners incarcerated -- the war was over, but the bondage continued. One day an Allied plane landed in a field near the prison and through the fence that surrounded the compound, an airman informed the General of the Japanese's surrender and the American victory. Wainwright immediately pulled his emaciated body to attention, turned and marched toward the command house, burst through the door, marched up to the camp's commanding officer and said, "My Commander-in-Chief has conquered your Commander-in-Chief. I am now in charge of this camp." In response to Wainwright's declaration, the officer took off his sword, laid it on the table, and surrendered his command. (Spiritual Strongholds, Don McMinn, Oklahoma City OK, 1993).

There is absolutely nothing you can do to make these things true in your life. They are already true. God has done it. Bondage is over and the prison doors have been opened wide. Will you believe God and by faith walk through them and experience the freedom Christ has purchased for you? "It is for freedom that Christ has set us free. Stand firm, then, and do not let yourselves be burdened again by a yoke of slavery" (Gal. 5:1).

Freedom is your birthright. Don't settle for less!!!

Made in the USA
Columbia, SC
23 September 2020